Ethics and Etiquette
For Today's Ministry

Terry R. Baughman
and Gayla M. Baughman

WWW.BAUGHMANGROUP.ORG

ETHICS AND ETIQUETTE
For Today's Ministry

Terry R. Baughman
and Gayla M. Baughman

ISBN 978-0-9710411-7-2

Published by: Baughman Group Ministries
                PO Box 2030
                Gilbert, AZ 85299
                480.381.5016
                Email: trbaughman@baughmangroup.org
                Website: www.baughmangroup.org

Printed by: Morris Publishing
                Kearney, NE 68847
                800.650.7888

Contents

To our parents
You believed in us

Acknowledgements

We are a product of all who have influenced our lives, but to mention the names of each would fill this book and there would be no room left for text. Suffice it to say that we gratefully acknowledge the multitude of teachers, preachers, relatives, and friends who have blessed our lives and shaped our understanding of the principles that we write about.

Most importantly, we acknowledge our parents to whom this book is dedicated, AJ and Geraldine Baughman of Fayetteville, Arkansas, and Pastor Robert J. and Elaine Bibb of Phoenix, Arizona, from whom the seeds of ethics were sown and continue to be nurtured in us. They raised us to believe that ethics and Christianity were inseparable and the most important thing to do is the *right* thing. They are the true authors of this book.

Heartfelt thanks and genuine appreciation is in order for those who have assisted in the editing and preparation for publication of this manuscript. Again, Nancy Hunt has given hours of time to read and edit the manuscript, catching multiple grammatical errors and suggesting ways to make the message clearer. Also, thanks to Violet Moore for her insightful edits and thoughtful suggestions to perfect the printed page.

Josh Rivas has demonstrated his talent with graphic arts in the cover design and layout. Thanks for using your talents for God and sharing them with us.

We also acknowledge our students at *Christian Life College* who have caused us to reach for more understanding with their multitude of questions. We have been challenged, strengthened, and encouraged by the opportunity to instruct you and in turn we have been taught. You compel us to excel.

Special thanks to our Lord and Savior Jesus Christ who has given us the passion to pursue His calling. We would be nothing without Him. All our efforts are to bring glory to His name.

Terry & Gayla Baughman

Scripture References

Scripture references in *Ethics & Etiquette for Today's Ministry* are from the translations or paraphrases listed below. In the various quotations we have emphasized words or phrases with *italics*. It should be understood that this is the emphasis of the authors and not of the original translation or paraphrase. The assortment of translations selected is to bring greater understanding and clarity to the passages of Scripture. Where a version is not specified, scriptural quotations are from the New King James Version of The Holy Bible. Acknowledgement is here made to the various translations and their copyright owners with appreciation for the fair use inclusion in this work:

NKJ - *New King James Version of the Holy Bible,* copyright 1982 Thomas Nelson, Inc.

KJV - *King James Version,* The Authorized Version of the Holy Bible is in the public domain.

MSG - *The Message,* copyright 1993, 1994, 1995, 1996, 2000, 2001, 2002 by Eugene H. Peterson.

NASB - *New American Standard Bible,* copyright 1960, 1962, 1963, 1968, 1971, 1972, 1973, 1975, 1977, 1995 by The Lockman Foundation.

NCV - *New Century Version,* the Holy Bible, copyright 1987, 1988, 1991 by Word Publishing, Dallas TX.

NIV - *New International Version,* copyright 1973, 1978, 1984 by International Bible Society.

NLT - *New Living Translation Holy Bible,* copyright 1996 by Tyndale Charitable Trust.

NRSV - *New Revised Standard Version of the Bible,* copyright 1989, by the Division of Christian Education of the National Council of Churches of Christ in the U.S.A.

TLB - *The Living Bible* is an English version of the Bible by Kenneth Taylor released in 1971, Tyndale House.

Preface

It is a daunting task to write a book, especially a book on *ethics and etiquette*. Once written, the evidence is recorded for all generations to judge you by your own words. Pilate must have felt that preponderance of permanence, when he said of the inscription he ordered to be affixed to the cross, "What I have written, I have written."

When you publish a book on etiquette, everyone assumes you are always prim and proper. When you write about ethics, it is assumed you are always ethical and emulate the paragon of perfect conduct. Neither is true of the authors of this book. We reserve the right to make mistakes!

However, we have seen the need to produce this work on *ethics and etiquette* to be a guide, a sourcebook of material for pastors, a textbook for students, and an encouragement to all who aspire to ministry. The ministry is comprised of imperfect people who have a passion, a desire to model Christ to the world and to share His message. In our desire to be the finest purveyors of the gospel we must give attention to our personal conduct to be the very best that we can be. The apostle Paul challenges us,

> Be an example to the believers in word, in conduct, in love, in spirit, in faith, in purity. ... Give attention to reading, to exhortation, to doctrine. ... Meditate on these things; give yourself entirely to them, that your progress may be evident to all (1 Timothy 4:12-13, 15).

We offer the following credentials as evidence of our experience in ministry and as a backdrop for many of the principles and practices taught in this book. It is not our intention to bring honor or accolades to ourselves for any accomplishments recorded here, only to demonstrate an understanding of ministerial ethics from a broad base of personal experiences.

Terry R. Baughman is a minister of the *United Pentecostal Church International*, first licensed in 1976, then ordained in 1980 by the Arkansas District. He has been a member of the UPCI in five districts: Arkansas, Texas, Texico (West Texas & New Mexico), Arizona, and Western (California & Nevada) Districts. He has held a number of district offices including: Sunday School Secretary (Texico), Youth President (AZ), and Home Missions Director (AZ). He has been on staff at Christian Life College since 1994, serving in various capacities: Campus Pastor, Dean of Students, Academic Dean, and Executive Vice President.

Gayla M. Baughman was raised in a pastor's home in Pocatello, Idaho. She began evangelizing with her family, *The Bible Singing Bibb Family,* in 1975. Much of her early ministry was in songwriting and recording. She now devotes her time to writing and ladies ministries. Gayla was appointed to serve on the Women of the Word commission of the UPCI in 2002. She has contributed to the popular *More to Life* Bible studies for women. She serves as the advisor for the western region *Open Door* conference and is a member of the Ladies Ministries committee of the Western District UPCI.

Together we have evangelized (9 years), served as assistant pastor and music directors (1 year), pastored three churches (2 of which we planted), and taught in Christian Life College since 1994. *We now write books together!*

1

Introduction

We give no offense in anything,
that our ministry may not be blamed.
—2 Corinthians 6:3

The subject of ethics is often in the news. Politicians
and priests, business executives and television
personalities are called into question for their
violations of ethical conduct. Politicians have been brought
before ethics panels to question their business practices or
personal pandering. Priests practicing pedophilia have been
an embarrassment to the Catholic Church. Enron and
WorldCom became case studies of ethics gone wrong in
corporate America. News anchors have been humiliated
for politically-biased reporting of inaccurate news stories,
and plagiarizing reporters have been taken to task for their
errant journalism.

There is a crisis of ethics in contemporary culture.
Postmodernity has embraced a double standard of

expectation. In a tolerant society excuses are often made for almost any transgression, then when the misdeed becomes excessive or the wrongdoer appears in the public view, great consternation is expressed and dismay over the breach of proper conduct. It is very difficult to be non-judgmental on one hand and then espouse a standard of ethical behavior on the other. Adhering to moral absolutes in one breath and professing to be broadminded about human sexuality in another is a conflict of values. It is an impossible oxymoron of ethics, a deception of conviction.

Regardless of the condition of ethics in culture or the corporate setting, there must always be a superior standard of conduct for Christians. Professing Christians are called to a higher level of ethics. Inherently, people know that Christians are supposed to be people of conviction, moral behavior, and proper conduct. When they are not, there is shock and the credibility of all Christians suffer as a result.

Even more so, ministers of the Christian faith are under the microscope of inspection. At the least bit of questionable conduct the news hounds are alerted and the howling is heard far and wide. If for no other reason than the potential embarrassment of exposure, the conduct of the minister must be held to the highest standards of ethical integrity.

Often in ministry there will be situations where *ethics* are the guiding criteria for a proper response. Ministers and people involved in the ministry of the church should adhere to the highest standard of personal integrity and professional ethics.

Ethics & Etiquette Defined

By definition *ethics* is the study of standards of conduct and moral judgment. It is also understood to be the system of morals of a person, religion, or a professional group, as in *medical ethics* for health care professionals or *business ethics* for those in corporate groups. So, any standard of conduct adopted by an individual, group, or association can be defined as *ethics*—sometimes called a "code of ethics." It is an accepted standard of proper behavior.

On the other hand, *etiquette* is rules of behavior to define acceptable conduct in the social context. Having a good code of ethics leads to good moral behavior; practicing proper etiquette results in good social conduct.

The principles of ministerial ethics are an outgrowth of godly character, where the rules of etiquette govern acceptable social behavior. Etiquette is about good manners, while ethics dictate good moral judgment.

> **Etiquette is about good manners, while ethics dictate good moral judgment.**

Biblical principles of morality are not subject to debate, nor are they designed to be negotiable by some conference drawing up a *code of ethics*. Therefore, the effort to develop a study of ethics and etiquette has more to do with good behavior and proper conduct in areas that may not be specifically addressed in

Scripture. Morality will be addressed, not as though it was optional, but rather to stress the vital importance of moral purity in the lives of anyone who strives for ministry.

Is it any wonder, as our culture moves away from the moorings of morality, that ethics have no anchor to hold our values?

Professional Ethics

Those in the medical profession have long subscribed to a professional code of ethics referred to as the *Hippocratic Oath*. It was named for the ancient Greek physician Hippocrates and has undergone various revisions during the last 2,000 years. Many medical schools have adopted some version of the oath, which is accepted and affirmed by each graduating class. One version approved by the American Medical Association follows:

*You do solemnly swear, each by whatever he or
she holds most sacred
That you will be loyal to the Profession of
Medicine and just and generous to its members
That you will lead your lives and practice your
art in uprightness and honor
That into whatsoever house you shall enter, it
shall be for the good of the sick to the utmost of
your power, your holding yourselves far aloof
from wrong, from corruption, from the
tempting of others to vice
That you will exercise your art solely for the
cure of your patients, and will give no drug,
perform no operation, for a criminal purpose,
even if solicited, far less suggest it*

*That whatsoever you shall see or hear of the
lives of men or women which is not fitting to
be spoken, you will keep inviolably secret
These things do you swear. Let each bow the
head in sign of acquiescence
And now, if you will be true to this, your oath,
may prosperity and good repute be ever yours;
the opposite, if you shall prove yourselves
forsworn.*[1]

Medical ethics are intended to preserve life and to practice the art in such a way as to bring cures and health to the patient. In the current cultural climate it is not surprising that even longstanding principles of ethics in the medical community are changing. Traditional ethics are being challenged by new medical practitioners who justify the termination of life based on a new criterion—*quality of life*, rather than the value of life.

A medical doctor in the state of Michigan, Jack Kevorkian (dubbed Dr. Death), was embroiled in controversy because he championed the cause of assisted suicide to those who were terminally ill and came to him for assistance in ending their lives. After assisting over 100 patients in suicide, Kevorkian was charged and convicted of second degree murder in 1999 for illegally assisting the suicide of Thomas Youk.[2]

---

[1]"Hippocratic Oath," *Microsoft Encarta Encyclopedia 2000.* ©1993-1999 Microsoft Corporation. All rights reserved.

[2] Frontline: *The Kevorkian Verdict;* ©1995-2005 WGBH Educational Foundation; online; accessed June 19, 2005; available from http://www.pbs.org/wgbh/pages/frontline/kevorkian/chronology.html.

Jack Kevorkian, who lost his medical license as a result of his activity in assisted suicide, is the exception rather than the rule. Most doctors continue to conscientiously perform their practice with allegiance to an established code of ethics.

Occasionally you may hear of politicians or other professional people being questioned by an ethics panel. Why are ethics questioned when there is no criminal wrongdoing? Though there may be nothing illegal (against the law) in what they have done, there is an ethical standard that has been violated. Professionals in many vocations are expected to live up to a "code of ethics," a statement of professional conduct, either written or unwritten.

Newt Gingrich became Speaker of the House of Representatives in 1995 after rising through the ranks in the political arena. Through his "Contract with America" he was credited for being the catalyst of change that put the Republicans in power of both the House and Senate in the elections of 1994. Seven years prior to this history moment, in 1987, Gingrich initiated ethics charges against Jim Wright, Speaker of the House. Ironically, he was himself called before the House Ethics Committee in 1996. He was reprimanded for failing to register his political action committee, giving the committee false information, and using tax-exempt donations for political activities. The House disciplined Gingrich for his ethics violations and fined him $300,000. He was reelected, but in the wake of controversy chose to resign.

Former President Bill Clinton was called into question over his ethics. He was impeached by the Congress for immoral behavior with a White House intern, Monica Lewinsky. The Senate stopped short of removing him from office. He maintained that his private moral life should be disassociated from his professional life.

Corporate business leaders have been investigated for questionable business practices. Some large corporations have squandered the retirement savings of their employees while padding their own pocketbooks. Company executives of Enron Corporation were indicted for wrongdoing and some served jail sentences. After the financial collapse of WorldCom, CEO Bernard Ebbers was sentenced to twenty-five years in prison for what prosecutors said was the largest securities fraud in history. Five other former executives were implicated for their involvement in the fraud.

In the last few years, a major scandal ripped the Catholic Church as a flood of accusations became public over the immoral practices of priests who were guilty of pedophilic practices and involved in homosexual behavior. More than 200 priests resigned or were dismissed from duties in the nationwide investigation. From Boston, Cincinnati, Phoenix, San Francisco and other cities, victims of abuse began to come forward and tell their woeful tales of mistreatment at the hands of the clergy.

One such priest, John J. Geoghan of Boston, Massachusetts, was accused of fondling or raping more than 130 children in over thirty years of parish ministry.[3] He served time in prison, all the while maintaining his innocence, until he was strangled to death by a fellow inmate.

While we may excuse ourselves saying, "Well, that's the Catholic Church," we must be aware that abuse, infidelity, immoral conduct, and criminal acts have been committed by ministers of all denominations and affiliations. No one is above the law and temptation comes to everyone. Scandal can mar the good name of the church when members of the clergy forget their responsibility as a moral force in the community and as leaders of righteousness.

Ministers of the gospel must never yield to culture's pressure to abandon absolutes in areas of morality and ethics. While moral conduct may be redefined by a tolerant society and ethical rules are discarded by politicians, corporate leaders, and even religious representatives, the God-called minister must strive to maintain the highest moral virtue and live a life of absolute integrity.

The Minister's Calling

The minister of the gospel must approach the ministry with certainty. You cannot vacillate in your

---

[3] Azcentral.com, *Abuse in the Catholic Church: Special Report*, online; accessed June 22, 2005; available from http://www.azcentral.com/news/church/priestindex.html.

decision to pursue the ministry; it is vital to know your calling. There will be times when you will question your call, while in the heat of battle or in the aftermath of depression. In those times you must have a deep conviction that you are called of God and you are following His holy urge.

Not everyone has the same experience in his calling. Some may hear a voice or see a vision, while others may just sense a deep drawing of the Spirit to ministry. There are those, like Nehemiah, who have merely responded to a need, only to find themselves in the center of God's work without really planning to enter the ministry. Regardless of the circumstances that brought you into the ministry, you must have a conviction that God's will is the most important thing in life and you are pursuing Him.

Several of the Old Testament prophets experienced an identifiable call, a magnificent moment, an incredible vision, or a divine compulsion. Isaiah saw the Lord on the throne, accompanied by winged seraphim, in a splendid display of God's eternal presence. His call came in the form of a question, "Whom shall I send and who will go?" Isaiah quickly responded, "Here I am Lord, Send me!"

Jeremiah was called before he was born. God said, "Before I formed you in the womb I knew you; Before you were born I sanctified you; I ordained you a prophet to the nations" (Jeremiah 1:5). With that sense of destiny he was able to fulfill a difficult ministry of rejection and scorn. He saw himself as "a man of contention to the whole earth" (Jeremiah 15:10), but he was faithful throughout more than forty years of ministry and was an eyewitness to the destruction of Jerusalem that he had long prophesied.

Through the experience of Jeremiah, you can be assured that God already knows the vocation for which you are uniquely qualified. He knows your abilities and disabilities. When He called you, He did so knowing you just as you are. When He calls, it is not just an assignment or an occupation, it is your life! His call says, *"I appointed you — You have a job to do!"*

Amos was a farmer, a man from the fields. He said, "I was no prophet. Nor was I a son of a prophet, But I was a sheepbreeder and a tender of sycamore fruit. Then the LORD took me as I followed the flock, and the LORD said to me, 'Go, prophesy to My people Israel.'" (Amos 7:14-15).

When God calls, our background or lack of pedigree is immaterial. Our handicaps become assets. Our deficiency becomes an occasion for His sufficiency. Our need becomes an opportunity for His enablement! Never glory in ignorance nor brag about a lack of education; rather apply yourself to learning and rely on the Spirit of God to prepare you for the task of ministry.

The calling of God is a call to action. It is never a call to sit, but to arise. It is not a call to stay, but to go! Moses ran from danger in Egypt to the security of a deserted desert. He built his new life in the shelter of obscurity and the comfort of anonymity. But God knew where he was and used the desert place to prepare a future leader. A spiritual encounter in an out-of-the-way place, a prophetic voice from the burning bush, translated to a burning purpose for his life. He would never be the same.

Moses was taken from his safe shelter of obscurity to the center stage of Pharaoh's palace in Egypt with a divine directive, "Let my people go!" It takes a definite call to inspire such bold assertiveness. When the call of God is cemented in your heart and the message is confirmed in your spirit, there is a confident boldness in your ministry.

Our handicaps become assets. Our deficiency becomes an occasion for His sufficiency!

Elijah fared well in the showdown on Mount Carmel but caved in to depression in the aftermath of his greatest victory. He made the journey from obscurity (during the years of drought), to public notoriety (on Mount Carmel), then to running for his life! Jezebel threatened revenge for the slaying of the prophets of Baal. In the midst of despair he cried out to God, "I'm the only one left and I'm about to die." God's answer was a slight rebuke and a shocking revelation, "I've got 7,000 who have never bowed a knee to Baal. Now, go anoint a successor to your ministry!" (See 1 Kings 19.)

Just when you think you are the only one doing the work of God and can never be replaced ... think again!

God loves you and will use you in the greatest calling on earth, but it is *His* work and *His* ministry and someday, someone else will take your place!

Wear the mantle well. Be an honorable representative of the calling that God has placed on you. When the day arrives for you to take your heavenly flight, the mantle of ministry will fall on the shoulders of a servant in the next generation.

The mantle of ministry is a regal robe and a wearisome weight.

The mantle of ministry is a regal robe and a wearisome weight. Sometimes you speak with such anointing and power that you feel as though you were Moses on Mount Sinai delivering the message of God from a personal revelation. Other times you wear the weight of ministry like a ball and chain, delivering a difficult message with the burden of Jeremiah. You can love it and you can hate it, but never dishonor it.

The following verse was used by Joe E. Trull and James E. Carter in an excellent book, *Ministerial Ethics: Moral Formation for Church Leaders*. From the classic *Canterbury Tales,* this verse speaks to the contemporary issue of ethical conduct in ministry:

Wide was his parish, houses far asunder,
But never did he fail, for rain or thunder,
In sickness, or in sin, or any state,
To visit to the farthest, small and great,

Going afoot, and in his hand a stave.
This fine example to his flock he gave,
That first he wrought and afterwards he taught;
Out of the gospel then that text he caught,
And this figure he added thereunto—
That, if gold rust, what shall poor iron do?
For if the priest be foul, in whom we trust,
What wonder if a layman yield to lust?
                    --Geoffrey Chaucer, Canterbury Tales[4]

Of all the classes I have taught at Christian Life College, there is none more vital than the course in *Ministerial Ethics*. The majority of students may never make great preachers. They may be adequate ministers at best, with limited knowledge of the Pentateuch or the mechanics of homiletics. They may fail in their interpretation of the parables or confuse the events in the Historical Books, but they dare not fail in honesty, morality, and ministerial responsibility.

Every time I approach the class in *Ministerial Ethics*, I do so seriously and with passion, knowing that the students I teach today will be leaders in ministry tomorrow. Their success and continued integrity may depend on the principles of ethical conduct I can drill into them in one brief hour each week during the semester. The haunting words of Chaucer challenge me: *"For if the priest*

---

[4] Geoffrey Chaucer, *Canterbury Tales* in *Ministerial Ethics: Moral Formation for Church Leaders,* by Joe E. Trull and James E. Carter, (Grand Rapids: Baker Academic, 2004).

be foul, in whom we trust, what wonder if a layman yield to lust?"

The call to be a minister of the Lord Jesus Christ places demands upon the individual that surpass every other vocation. Of all professions, the ministry must uphold the highest ideals of integrity and ethics.

2

Personal Conduct in Ministry

*I write so that you may know how you
ought to conduct yourself in the house of God,
which is the church of the living God,
the pillar and ground of the truth.*
—1 Timothy 3:15

One student in a *Ministerial Ethics* class at Christian Life College asked the question, "Why do we need to develop a code of ethics to live by? If people love Jesus and are in a right relationship with God, shouldn't they always do the right thing?"

While essentially the premise of the question was correct, I reminded the class that even two Spirit-filled Christians, who are living for God, may often encounter conflicts in their relationships. There must be a code of conduct, an ethical procedure that will guide them to make right decisions and develop proper action in their relational experiences.

A proper conduct in ministry will be the outgrowth of many and varied relationships. Consider the vital relationships each minister finds himself in, beginning with himself, then working outwardly to his spouse, family, friends, church members and other associations. Of course, the highest in importance is the minister's personal relationship with God.

Right Relationship with Self

Before one can develop proper relationships with others, he must have a right relationship with himself. That may seem a little odd since most of us have been taught to think more of others and little of self. It is certainly inappropriate for one "to think of himself more highly than he ought to think" (Romans 12:3), but there is a healthy balance of positive self-image that is necessary. How well do you know yourself?

"Hello Me, my name is *Self*. How are you? I would like to get to know *Me* better."

This may sound a little strange if you were trying to introduce yourself to yourself. But I would venture to say that some people need to be introduced to the person they really are. Once they get to know who they are, they will better understand how to have a healthy self-image.

The Gospel of Matthew gives us a healthy perspective on the important order of relationships. In the context, Jesus responds to the question concerning which are the greatest of the commandments. His twin assignment of priority includes a relationship with self.

16

"Teacher, which is the great commandment in the law?" Jesus said to him, *"You shall love the LORD your God with all your heart, with all your soul, and with all your mind."* This is the first and great commandment. And the second is like it: *"You shall love your neighbor as yourself."* On these two commandments hang all the Law and the Prophets (Matthew 22:36-40).

The first and most important relationship is with the Lord your God. Loving Him with all your heart, soul and mind is a commandment. It is not an option or a multiple choice answer in a relationship exam. The second is like it, or in other words, just as important. It stands on the same rung of the ladder with the first one. "Love your neighbor as yourself."

> **The first and most important relationship is with the Lord your God.**

The Bible does not leave any consideration that someone would not love himself. It is a given—an understood factor hanging on the same rung with the first two. It seems to imply, "You love yourself; now love your neighbor with the same intensity!" The potential to love our neighbor as commanded is hampered if we do not love ourselves. You have no other choice; you are commanded to love yourself.

Self is the most familiar bond. Therefore, it is the first one with which we have the opportunity to reconcile.

17

We cannot successfully expand the sphere of relationships into the next community, that of our neighbor, until the closest one is resolved.

It is a difficult task to convince others to love themselves in the proper biblical fashion. People are either so damaged by dysfunctional relationships and inferiorities that they wear a shroud of guilt for even caring about themselves, or they have indulged in pride and arrogance to compensate for their insecurities. The pendulum swings wide in either direction to correct this problem of self-image. We find an abundance of materials, curriculum, and classes on the subject of "_self._" There are discussion groups for improving _self_-image, _self_-esteem counseling in schools, and an ever-expanding _self_-help section in the library. With all the materials that are available, people still struggle to develop a proper self-image.

But how can we convince others to love themselves when we wrestle with the self-love issue ourselves? Let us establish the fact that loving yourselves is expected. God loves us; He proved it at creation and confirmed it at Calvary. Let it not be said that we doubt His love. The first commandment is to return His love; love Him, with all your heart, soul and mind.

What about the second commandment? I must love my neighbor, or my brother, as myself. How can I love my brother like I love _me_ when I don't love _me_? Now that is something to think about! _I don't love me._ I don't hate me, because I take care of myself. I feed myself when I feel the first twinges of hunger. I am careful not to bang the hammer on my thumb again, because it hurt the first time and I don't want to hurt myself again. Now, isn't this love? Do I feel these things for others I love? I do not want them to be uncomfortable, or to hurt, because I love them. So cannot we deduct that the same emotional feelings that we have for those we love are similar to the ones we feel for ourselves?

A minister will struggle with all other relationships until he settles the self-love issue. Love yourself. Go ahead and accept it. See yourself as God sees you, a valuable priceless treasure worth dying for.

Take a few moments right now to spend some time in prayer. Ask God to help you accept His love as you should, so that you can accept yourself. One who remembers how he is loved, will indeed show love to others.

> **See yourself as God sees you, a valuable priceless treasure worth dying for.**

Right Relationship with Family

The next closest community in relationships is your family. Sadly, some have learned too late that you can't put church before family. You must make time for your family. *If you fail at home, what good have you accomplished?*

It is of great importance that the family is cared for first. The congregation will reap far greater benefits if the minister's family is happy and well taken care of. The minister's wife finds contentment when her husband is loving, attentive, and sensitive to her needs. The minister's children will be well-balanced and secure in their self identity with a father that takes time to invest in their lives.

A minister must work to keep the love alive in his relationship with his spouse. The Lord's work can become so intense that even when you come home, your mind is on the problems of the members in your congregation. After a difficult day of church problems, it takes a conscious effort to lay disturbing thoughts aside and engage in basic conversation with your wife when you come home. It may seem trivial, but the time you spend with her is valuable to the preservation of your relationship. In your well-meaning effort to help others, take care not to neglect the needs in your own marriage.

It is vital that the children receive the positive affirmation of being a part of the family unit. It is not one big happy family with the church; the home family unit must be preserved. A pastor once confided to me that one of the greatest disappointments of his life occurred one evening when he was called away from the supper table by a disgruntled member. As the pastor dutifully prepared to go meet with the member, one of his sons said, *"Dad has time for everyone but us!"*

Dr. Arlo Moehlenpah delivered a message at the Christian Life Center (Stockton, CA) men's retreat in 1996. He spoke of things he had learned too late about being a father to his children. In vulnerable honesty, he expressed regrets concerning things he would like to have done differently in raising his children. We would all like a second chance, but we must do our best the first time around. There are no second chances at childhood, parenting, or living.

Learn lessons from other's mistakes so you will not make the same errors with your kids. Joe E. Trull and James E. Carter, in *Ministerial Ethics: Moral Formation for Church Leaders*, said, "No other success compensates for failure in the home."[5]

When all is said and done and you look back on life in your sunset years, your family is your most important asset. In the book, *Seven Promises of a Promise Keeper*, one man said that at the end of life, "Few men ever express regret that they didn't earn more money or work longer at the office. But many state bitterly that they should have paid more attention to their families."[6]

Right Relationships with Friends

Beyond the circle of family there is the realm of friends. Who are your friends? Henry Durbanville won first prize for the best definition of a friend in a British publication. He wrote, "A friend is the first person who comes in when the whole world goes out."[7]

There are times in the ministry when it seems no one understands you. It can be very lonely when you feel you cannot confide in the church members and it seems the whole world has *gone out* and you are left alone to figure it all out.

---

[5] Joe E. Trull & James E. Carter, *Ministerial Ethics, Moral Formation for Church Leaders*, (Grand Rapids: Baker, 2004), 70.

[6] Al Janssen, ed., *Seven Promises of a Promise Keeper*, (Colorado Springs: Focus on the Family Publishing, 1994), 103.

[7] Sermons.Com., online; accessed June 21, 2005; available from http://www.christianglobe.com/ Illustrations/a-z/f/friendship. htm.

Everyone needs friends. It is a human need that can only be fulfilled by another. God created Adam and then observed, "It is not good that man should be alone." So, He made him a friend. Well, she was his lover too ... but I believe she was his first best friend.

It is a healthy sign if your spouse is your best friend, but if your spouse is your *only* friend, that can be unhealthy. You need others to balance out your opinions; someone with which to bounce around your ideas. Friends give you a rounded perspective of life. In a group of friends, your ideas become limitless. When you have friends, it is easier to choose someone you can trust for accountability.

Positive people make supportive friends.

When selecting friends, a minister ought to find those who will enhance his ministry. Friends that encourage should be sought out when you need an uplifting conversation. Positive people make supportive friends.

It is difficult to have close friends among the congregation. Although the group is filled with wonderful people with whom you get along, it is the wise pastor who is cautious about sharing problems with a member of his congregation. When a pastor singles out one person to be a best-friend, or prefers one's company over the other, it causes insecurities in the other church members. This opens the door for jealousy and other undesirable spirits to creep into the church. Since the welfare of the church is the pastor's responsibility, his choice of friends is critical and his abandon of partiality is beneficial to the congregation.

The best friends we have as a couple are other people that blend with our personalities. Many hours of quality fellowship can be spent with a couple that the husband and the wife enjoy equally.

It is good to make yourself available as a friend to people who do not share your faith, but it is a dangerous thing to isolate yourself from fellow believers and gravitate to those friends alone. There is nothing like sharing time with people of the same faith. They will encourage you, balance you, and pray for you when you are in need.

It may be necessary to seek out friends. Those with the most friends are those who show themselves friendly. Friends are worth the search. Initially, you may have to reach out to someone you would like to get to know, but once you cultivate a close friendship, the result is well worth the effort.

Right Relationships in Business

The majority of ministers are bi-vocational. In other words, they work two jobs—the ministry and some other occupation to make a living! The balance between secular and sacred is the most difficult responsibility the minister has. It is impossible to completely segregate these two areas of life. You are first of all a minister of the gospel. Whatever else you do, be it accounting, sanitation, or selling, will be in addition to the sacred call on your life.

Conduct of the man of God in the work place or among business associates will be vital to his success. The report we have among those who know us best is the true reflection of who we are. In the Scripture we are warned against slothfulness, and we are instructed to be diligent in business.

Be kindly affectioned one to another with brotherly love; in honour preferring one another; *Not slothful in business*; fervent in spirit; serving the Lord (Romans 12:10-11 KJV).

Where the text says "not slothful in business," the NKJ says, "not lagging in diligence." Our conduct on the job is a reflection of who we are as Christians. If we are frequently late, miss deadlines, make excuses, and conduct personal business while at work; we create a reputation for laziness, dishonesty, and a lack of productivity. If we are testifying about our Christianity and inviting people to our church, what kind of impression are we making concerning our lives as ministers, or even as Christians?

Guidelines for Personal Conduct

For this is the will of God, your sanctification: that *you should abstain from sexual immorality;* that each of you should know how to possess his own vessel in sanctification and honor, not in passion of lust, like the Gentiles who do not know God; that *no one should take advantage of and defraud his brother in this matter,* because the Lord *is* the avenger of all such, as we also forewarned you and

24

testified. *For God did not call us to uncleanness, but in holiness.* Therefore he who rejects this does not reject man, but God, who has also given us His Holy Spirit.

But concerning brotherly love you have no need that I should write to you, for *you yourselves are taught by God to love one another;* and indeed you do so toward all the brethren who are in all Macedonia. But we urge you, brethren, that you increase more and more; that *you also aspire to lead a quiet life, to mind your own business, and to work with your own hands,* as we commanded you, that you may *walk properly toward those who are outside,* and that you may lack nothing (1 Thessalonians 4:3-12).

Paul leaves us a long list of qualities that the Christian, and especially the minister, should strive to internalize. He says these things are the "will of God." This might not be what you really want to hear when you are seeking the "will of God," but until you get these basics of Christianity down, you need not seek the grand and lofty dreams of great feats in public ministry.

"Abstain from sexual immorality." Simple and straightforward, without excuses or dependency, or whining about victimization, Paul says, "Abstain." Give up your immorality. "Each of you should learn to control his own body in a way that is holy and honorable" (1 Thessalonians 4:4 NIV).

"Defraud not nor take advantage of your brother." A right relationship with God means you will have a right relationship with your brother. You cannot take advantage of your brother on Friday and then profess your love for God in the pulpit on Sunday. John gives us this insight,

> If someone says, "I love God," and hates his brother, he is a liar; *for he who does not love his brother whom he has seen, how can he love God whom he has not seen?* (1 John 4:20).

"God did not call us to uncleanness, but in holiness." We are *not* to lead lives that are impure, but dedicated lives to reflect the purity of God in us. A life of consecration to God will cause you to live a clean life.

"Love one another." Back to the basics; it is kindergarten time again. Paul is saying, I shouldn't have to bring this up, but we must love one another. It seems like this ought to be a *given*, an accepted and well understood principle of Scripture. Yet, we need to be reminded again, "By this all will know that you are My disciples, if you have love for one another" (John 13:35).

"Aspire to lead a quiet life." The NIV says, "Make it your ambition to lead a quiet life." In the erratic rat race of modern existence, it takes a genuine effort to find *quiet time*, to find a moment for meditation and contemplation, just some time to be able to *think* without cell phones, text messages, mass media, and noise.

"Mind your own business." Have you ever told someone this? At least, you must have been tempted to tell someone, "Mind your own business." Did you know you

were quoting Scripture? Paul leaves us this nugget of wisdom. It is good advice. We have enough to do just trying to take care of our own business. If we manage that, we have accomplished the important business.

"Work with your hands." There is no feeling of accomplishment like the creative work of our own hands. When you are able to finish a project, there is a sense of satisfaction that comes from completing a work of your own hands. Since the expulsion from the garden there has been an innate need in mankind to work, to earn a living, to sweat, to labor. We may complain about the work, but there is a sense of achievement when the day is done and the task is complete.

"Walk properly toward those who are without." Our lives are billboards revealing the character of our relationships. When our relationships are in their proper order we will walk ethically and circumspectly. In so doing "those who are without" will esteem you for your good name. The NIV sums it up like this, live "so that your daily life may win the respect of outsiders."

A good report is earned by ethical conduct and by providing for the needs of those in your care. A minister must work to provide for his family!

> But if anyone does not provide for his own, and *especially for those of his household,* he has denied the faith and is worse than an unbeliever (1 Timothy 5:8).

An Ethical Person is one with a Good Name

Having a good reputation is crucial in establishing your credibility in the community. What kind of report do you have on the job, among your friends, with your family and acquaintances?

Several men in Scripture are noted to be men with _good names_. They are listed here in the biblical setting where they are identified by their reputations. They were "well spoken of," those with a "good testimony," and a "good reputation." In other words, others spoke of them favorably, noting their honesty and integrity. It could be stated that they were ethical men. Following are several of these references. In each, the ethical character qualities are emphasized:

Cornelius

And they said, "Cornelius the centurion, a just man, one who fears God and _has a good reputation_ among all the nation of the Jews" (Acts 10:22).

Stephen

Therefore, brethren, seek out from among you seven _men of good reputation_, full of the Holy Spirit and wisdom, whom we may appoint over this business (Acts 6:3).

Timothy

He was well spoken of by the brethren who were at Lystra and Iconium (Acts 16:2).

Ananias

Then a certain Ananias, a devout man according to the law, *having a good testimony* with all the Jews who dwelt there (Acts 22:12).

Titus' Friend

And we have sent with him *the brother whose praise is in the gospel* throughout all the churches (2 Corinthians 8:18).

Demetrius

Demetrius has a good testimony from all, and from the truth itself. And we also bear witness, and you know that our testimony is true (3 John 1:12).

Analyze your ethical standards. Not always is something *right* or *wrong*, but is it a violation of your personal standard of conduct? What kind of reputation are you building among your peers?

The impression I have of some that attended Bible College when I did is no longer accurate. Some have developed real character and change in their lives. However, it is difficult to cast off the impressions formed thirty years ago and accept the fact that they have changed. On the other hand, others may be less ethical now than they were when I knew them in the past.

Consistency and faithfulness are hallmark traits of ethical conduct. Your ethics are reflected in what you ARE. The facade of what you would like others to think of you is overshadowed by the reality of your conduct.

A good name is to be chosen rather than great riches,
Loving favor rather than silver and gold (Proverbs
22:1).

A *good name* is better than precious ointment
(Ecclesiastes 7:1a).

Some of the greatest preachers who have left the
ministry failed in their personal lives long before their
failures in public ministry. Failure in public is preceded by
failure in private. Eventually,
whatever a person is will be
demonstrated in his conduct. He
will be able to mask his true
character in front of people only
for a time before the truth is
revealed.

> The facade of what you would like others to think of you is overshadowed by the reality of your conduct.

Personal integrity must
become vital to the individual for
he must face himself in the mirror
everyday. *Integrity* cannot become
an old-fashioned word and an
outdated quality. Basic integrity is
being the same inside and out. It is
being true to God, to others, and to
yourself. It is avoiding duplicity (lying to yourself) and
hypocrisy (lying to others).

There are three outstanding examples of integrity
found in the Scripture. Joseph, who maintained integrity
in the most adverse circumstances; Job, who remained
faithful in the loss of everything he valued; and Daniel,

30

who constantly served God in a heathen culture with nothing negative recorded about him. Take a look at these men:

Joseph

- He resisted the temptation of Potiphar's wife.

  "There is no one greater in this house than I, nor has he kept back anything from me but you, because you are his wife. *How then can I do this great wickedness, and sin against God?*" So it was, as she spoke to Joseph day by day, that he did not heed her, to lie with her *or* to be with her (Genesis 39:9-10).

- He maintained integrity, even in prison.

  The keeper of the prison did not look into anything that was under Joseph's authority, because *the LORD was with him; and whatever he did, the LORD made it prosper* (Genesis 39:23).

- He was recognized and promoted by Pharaoh.

  Then Pharaoh said to Joseph, "Inasmuch as God has shown you all this, *there is no one as discerning and wise as you.* You shall be over my house, and all my people shall be ruled according to your word; only in regard to the throne will I be greater than you" Genesis 41:39-40).

Job

- Blameless and upright, He feared God and avoided evil.

  There was a man in the land of Uz, whose name *was* Job; and *that man was blameless and upright,* and one who feared God and shunned evil (Job 1:1).

- He remained faithful to God in the devastation of his life.

  In all this *Job did not sin nor charge God with wrong* (Job 1:22).

- He never knew what God said about him.

  Then the LORD said to Satan, "Have you considered My servant Job, that *there is none like him on the earth, a blameless and upright man,* one who fears God and shuns evil? And *still he holds fast to his integrity,* although you incited Me against him, to destroy him without cause" (Job 2:3).

Daniel

- He had a flawless reputation with the king.

  Then Daniel was brought in before the king. The king spoke, and said to Daniel, "Are you that Daniel who is one of the captives from Judah, whom my father the king brought from Judah? *I have heard of you, that the Spirit of God is in you, and that light and understanding and excellent wisdom are found in you"* (Daniel 5:13-14).

- His enemies could find nothing with which to charge him.

  So the governors and satraps sought to find some charge against Daniel concerning the kingdom; but *they could find no charge or fault, because he was faithful; nor was there any error or fault found in him.* Then these men said, "We shall not find any charge against this Daniel unless we find *it* against him concerning the law of his God" (Daniel 6:4-5).

It may be a little intimidating to study men and women in Scripture that never seem to have an impossible challenge and always come out on top. However, it is important to note that everyone, whether in ancient times or in contemporary culture, must keep a guard on their hearts and minds in order to maintain proper personal conduct.

All will have their trials and occasionally may fail. All will be tempted and at times may yield to temptation. All need to be reminded of the grace of our Lord Jesus Christ and his desire to lead us back into a relationship with him. Maintain your personal integrity by constantly relying on the strength of the Spirit, and the gift of His grace.

3

Presentation in Ministry

Let your light so shine before men, that they may see your good works and glorify your Father in heaven.
—Matthew 5:16

Proper decorum and etiquette should be observed in the organization and arrangement of each public event. Care should also be given to insure that you conduct yourself respectfully and with dignity. Your appearance and conduct in public or in private is a reflection on your denomination, your local congregation, and upon you as a minister. Most of all, remember that you are a representative of God. Conduct yourself with integrity and dress appropriately for every occasion. Seek to improve your *public image* so that you will be most effective in your ministry.

Improving Your Presentation

Imitation may be the sincerest form of flattery, but when someone mimics you, it is usually the bad points that are emphasized. It is like a caricature; it accentuates your negative characteristics! Do not be dismayed when you are confronted with your distracting habits, but purpose to work toward changing them.

Remember to maintain *eye contact* with the listener when speaking. This will help people stay focused on your message. Have you ever talked with someone who constantly looked away while you talked? Did you feel that he was uninterested in what you had to say? Communication is enhanced when you focus your attention on those to whom you are speaking. Whether preaching or in conversation, practice the positive habit of communicating with good eye contact.

> Practice the positive habit of communicating with good eye contact.

Speak distinctly and with sufficient volume. When words are slurred, mumbled, or even screamed it is sometimes difficult to understand what is being said. The purpose of preaching is to communicate a message. If you cannot be understood, you have failed to communicate. If you are timid or quiet it will appear that you are fearful or hesitant to declare your message. Practice speaking clearly and with sufficient volume so that all can understand your message.

Avoid distractions from your message. Your appearance, speech, mannerisms, and grooming affect your message. Think of times when you were so distracted by what someone was wearing that you failed to listen to the message. Your high fashion, or extreme lack of it, may limit your effectiveness.

Be the best you can be and always look for ways to improve your speech, your preaching, and your communication of the message. Some physical characteristics cannot be helped and may be compensated for in some other way.

Alan Oggs was a highly respected minister who spoke with distinction, overcoming a physical handicap of cerebral palsy. He was featured several times on James Dobson's *Focus on the Family* with his classic message: *You gotta have the want to!* It was an autobiographical, third-person account of his struggle to overcome handicaps in order to be a public speaker. In spite of his physical limitation he excelled in preaching and even had young ministers try to mimic his unique presentation!

Appearance

Recent studies have shown that a person's appearance has an affect on one's social image. By simply observing the clothing and appearance one can often identify an individual's economic status, relevance to style, and even moral aptitude. How an individual appears to others speaks words without uttering a sound; conveys volumes without a single letter being transcribed to a manuscript. As a minister, what does your appearance say to those who are under your leadership? What message are you conveying to the unbeliever in your city? How does the way you dress affect your effectiveness?

In the Bible College where we teach, the required dress code is one way of making the student aware of his/her appearance at all times. The dress code emphasizes the importance of being able to *dress up* for needed occasions and makes one more comfortable in dress attire.

Most areas of the country no longer expect a minister to dress in a suit and tie, except for purely official business. Be sensitive to your local culture. In some areas of the country, a preacher can wear blue jeans, boots, and a cowboy hat and fit right in!

Florence Littauer, author and seminar speaker on the personality temperaments commented in her book, *It Takes So Little To Be Above Average*, "A leader must wear the clothing of a leader."[8] There is an undeniable connection between the position an individual holds and the presentation that is made by his or her dress.

Aaron was the first high priest to serve in the tabernacle. God commanded special clothing to be made for him, citing two important reasons: first for *glory* and secondly, for *beauty*.

And you shall make holy garments for Aaron your brother, *for glory and for beauty*. So you shall speak to all who are gifted artisans, whom I have filled with the spirit of wisdom, that they may

---

[8] Florence Littauer, *It Takes So Little To Be Above Average* (Eugene, OR: Harvest House, 1984), 110.

make Aaron's garments, to consecrate him, that he may minister to Me as priest (Exodus 28:2-3).

The *New Living Translation* (NLT) renders this passage, "Make special clothes for Aaron to indicate his separation: beautiful garments that will lend dignity to his work." The clothing and appearance of a minister will either add dignity to his office or detract from his respectability.

Dress for Glory

The first reason for detailed instructions in the construction of Aaron's garments was for glory, to indicate his separation from the other people. The ministry is a vocation that is set apart from every other vocation on earth. In an analogy, the CEO is God; the company is His kingdom; the co-workers are apostles, prophets, evangelists, pastors, and teachers; the product is the gospel, and the customers are those to whom we are presenting our product. The employee's appearance is what sets him apart from other vocations. One working for God must be consecrated unto Him. His appearance must be modest, conservative, and a gentle reminder to the *customer* that he is not conformed to this world.

> The clothing and appearance of a minister will either add dignity to his office or detract from his respectability.

And do not be *conformed to this world*, but be transformed by the renewing of your mind, that you may prove what is that good and acceptable and perfect will of God (Romans 12:2).

Dress for Beauty

The second reason for making special garments for Aaron was for beauty. God wants you to be the best you can be. Represent God's company with tasteful, attractive clothing that will give honor and credence to His *Company*, and add dignity to your work.

The High Priest was obviously a very important job. God gave detailed instructions on how to construct the clothing from the undergarments to the outer coverings. Whenever God gave detailed instructions, there was purpose in the particulars.

Another instance where God gave specific instructions for construction was the tabernacle itself. Somehow, I believe this is related. The clothing the priest wore was equally important to the place where he fulfilled his purpose. God created this world down to the exact detail of every blade of grass, every grain of sand. Could it be that the clothing we wear while *on the job*, fulfilling His purpose, is just as important as the world in which we work? It should be that when people see us, they identify us with *the company*.

Aaron's clothes were intended to represent the importance of his position, to lend dignity to his work. The way a minister dresses, whether a man or a woman, makes a statement to those around him or her.

If you were given a prestigious job, you would not wear something wrinkled, dirty, or mismatched to work. If you see your position as important, you take pride in your appearance, thus giving credence to your work. The value of one's occupation is suspect if one's appearance is disheveled. On the other hand, nice, clean, attractive clothes add dignity to your job, just as it did with Aaron. Whatever your position is in the Kingdom of God, it is important. Wear clothes that add dignity to your work and value to your occupation.[9]

The Uniform

Many companies have dress codes for their employees. If you desire to work in law enforcement, you are identified as an authentic police officer when you are allowed to wear the uniform. While cadets are in training, they are not allowed to wear their uniforms in public. Upon graduation from the academy and their commissioning as a peace officer, they are given the privilege to wear their uniforms in public for the first time. When I see a policeman, I am reminded of this procedure and I know that this person has been trained and is qualified to wear the uniform.

The various branches of the military require their personnel to wear uniforms. Most fast food restaurants require uniforms, as well as hospital employees, delivery drivers, and city sanitation workers, just to name a few. A suit and tie could be seen as a uniform for a banker or an attorney.

---

[9] Ibid.

41

The word *uniform* should not be distasteful. A uniform is a distinctive outfit intended to identify those who wear it as members of a specific group. It is a good thing to be identified as a member of Jesus Christ's *company*.

Presenting a Standard

If you are a minister, minister's spouse, or other leader, those you mentor will tend to live just under your standards. Others will see a boundary in your life and set their sights on that goal. Fewer still will surpass your standards as a leader. Your moral principles and modesty standards may be faithfully proclaimed in the pulpit and lived consistently in your lifestyle, but those you hope to influence will usually live just shy of those expectations. Encourage higher standards in others by exceeding those expectations in your own personal disciplines.

Gender Specific Presentation

A female minister must be very careful about how she presents herself. A woman is often judged more harshly on her appearance, especially in the role of ministry. She must remember she is a lady, and liberty is given to those who submit to authority. If she remembers these three things, she will likely be more successful in her delivery of the message.

- **Be feminine.** Remember you are first a lady, and secondly a preacher. If you keep this order, gentlemen will respect you and listen to what you have to say.

- **Be modest.** Remember you are on an elevated platform and your hemline may look shorter from the pew. If you are appropriately covered at all times, no one should be able to question your intentions or the sincerity of your ministry.

- **Be confident, yet meek.** You do not need to be fearful of your calling nor intimidated by others. Confidence is needed to speak successfully on difficult topics. When confidence is mixed with an abundance of meekness, it will help you avoid arrogance and self-aggrandizement.

Presentation on a Budget

It is important to take note of the culture and social status of the people in your church. In other words, if you pastor a church where the people cannot afford to wear expensive clothing, you would make them feel uncomfortable if you were over-dressed. Yet on the other hand, if you dress on a modest budget, and yet look nicer than the people around you, it may be that you can teach them how to dress a step above with their meager incomes. The same garment that is clean and pressed looks more expensive than when it is stained and wrinkled.

Shopping for pre-worn clothing is a way to find quality clothes at a modest price. Consignment shops carry clean, name-brand clothes that are substantially lower in price than most department stores. Sales and close-out bargains are other ways to find good quality clothing without breaking your pocketbook. In most cases, it is better to buy one quality garment than several cheap changes. With quality comes durability and the garment will last longer; thus quality is more economical in the long run.

There is nothing wrong with looking your best. It is true that beauty should not depend solely upon outward adornment, yet the virtuous woman in Proverbs was clothed in tapestries and fine fabrics.

> She is not afraid of snow for her household, For all *her household is clothed with scarlet.* She makes tapestry for herself; *Her clothing is fine linen and purple* (Proverbs 31:21-22).

This woman also dressed her family and servants in good quality clothing. She did this not only to keep them warm but also to represent the status of her husband, who was known in the gates and sat among the elders of the land. She did not want to bring reproach on her husband who was much respected among other men. It is always good to remind ourselves that we represent someone other than ourselves. Whether it is a company we work for, a school we attend, or a church we pastor, people will look at the discipline of our appearance as a representation of the institution we are associated with. More importantly, as Christians we represent Christ to this world. It is good to take inventory of the way you dress. Those who look to you for leadership will model your good taste and modest apparel. You are an ambassador of your Savior, and you represent Him to those who see you in this world.

Business vs. Casual

Should a pastor wear a suit or fishing gear when he goes to the hospital? When is it proper to wear a casual shirt, open at the neck, and khaki pants? There is a time and place for each style, from business apparel to casual attire. You would not be expected to paint the bedroom in a suit you wear to church. Neither should you wear your paint clothes to church or to the grocery store. The casual versus business debate continues.

In an online article by Mary Ellen Guffey, the casual apparel dilemma is discussed in regards to the secular work environment. Guffey claims that one's choice of work clothes sends a strong nonverbal message to others. It also affects the way one works. Many employers have mixed feelings about the current trend toward increasingly casual business attire. They are concerned about the impact casual dress has on the overall morale of the company. As a general consensus, absenteeism, tardiness, and flirtatious behavior have increased as a result of the dress-down appearance, and customers are often turned off by casually-dressed employees.[10] As a result companies that once encouraged "casual Fridays" are cutting back on casual attire, in an effort to create a more professional image and conservative business climate.[11]

---

[10] Mary Ellen Guffey, *Business Communication Resources: The Perils of Casual Apparel in the Workplace*; online; accessed June 9, 2005; available from http://www.westwords.com/GUFFEY/liteplus/casual.html.

[11] Howard Lachtman, "Too Casual," The Stockton Record, September 27, 2002.

Some educational institutions that traditionally require a dress code have experimented with "casual days," allowing students to attend classes dressed in casual attire with mixed reviews. Other universities and colleges which have no official dress code are noticing a decline in school morale and attentiveness in class. Some secondary schools see dress attire as crucial to the educational process. They enforce a dress code as a way to prevent the wearing of *gang colors* or to impose a change on slovenly dressed students. Numerous public schools across the country have implemented the requirement of school uniforms. This is an initiative to counter-act the negative impact some casual attire has had in gang-infested areas.[12]

Some areas are more traditional while others are more casual.

It may make a difference where you intend to minister as to what you should wear. Hospital visitation is a good example of a place where you have the opportunity to represent the church to the community. While it does not require your *Sunday finest,* you should remember who you are representing.

Accepted protocol varies according to the region in which you pastor or minister. Some areas are more traditional while others are more casual. Ministers in rural farming communities will find public expectation much different than for those who

---

[12] Peter Caruso, "Individuality vs. Conformity: The Issue Behind School Uniforms." NASSP Bulletin 8 (September 1996), 581.

minister in urban centers with members of exceptional academic credentials. Local customs vary so take a cue from the local pastor when you are working as an assistant or an evangelist.

Many Christian colleges have student *dress codes* and guidelines of conduct as a part of their training in preparation for the ministry. These guidelines are intentionally conservative to train young men and women to look their best and to reflect an appropriate image for ministers in society. With this training they will be better prepared to adjust to business styles that are often expected of a member of the clergy. Some male students struggle with occasions where they are required to wear a suit and tie. Once they feel comfortable in more conservative dress clothes it is not such an issue, but it takes time. It is better to learn proper attire while in training, rather than make others uncomfortable in the *field* because you have been unable to adjust to the *uniform* of a minister.

Style and Fashion

Styles come and go. Fashions change as often as the seasons. Colors and lines change, suit lapels get wider or narrower; sometimes three-button suits are stylish and then they start modeling four. Should you buy double-breasted jackets or are they out of style? Shoes go from heels to flats, from tie-ups to slip-ons. It can be mind-boggling to keep up with the latest fashion.

Conservative styles reflect much less change. A conservative suit will always be in style. Conservative clothing fits into the center of each fashion strategy. It is the center of the road in the fashion freeway. It is a balance between wide lapels, and narrow ones, cropped sport coats and tails on a dinner jacket. It is the comfortable height of shoes between stilettos and flip-flops; the modest length dress between the thighs and the ankles; the well-groomed hair style somewhere between the unkempt spikes and the shaved head. Business professionals have led the way to prove that conservative dress is the professional *uniform*.

People will get the right message if you dress the right message.

What do your clothes say about you? If you dress sloppy, you may be saying that you are undisciplined, not only in your appearance, but in other areas of your life. What if you try to dress in clothes that clearly state a rebellious attitude or sport an anti-authority slogan printed on your t-shirt? Do you dress like a *player*, looking lustful and sending that message to the opposite sex? How about dressing modestly, conservatively, and godly? People will get the right message if you *dress* the right message.

Whether we like it or not, and whether it is right or wrong, people judge us by our appearance. The Bible is right once again with the statement: "Man looks on the outward appearance" (1 Samuel 16:7). Though God looks on our hearts, man can only judge us by what he sees. What message are we sending others by our appearance? Do our clothes reveal an attitude of indifference or a sense of responsibility? Are we sending a message of lust or of modesty, of disrespect or of reverence, of conformity to the world or of separation from it?[13]

There is no greater cause than the cause of Christ. The Bible does not specify a certain uniform but it does have some principles we should follow. There should be a definite distinction between the male and the female (Deuteronomy 22:5). We should always dress modestly (1 Timothy 2:9). Neither men nor women should wear clothing that is tight fitting or revealing. The loose morals of this world are evident in the suggestive clothing designed and modeled for current fashions. The influence of the homosexual agenda is evident in some of the fads that are popularly promoted, such as tight fitting, sensual styles for men, and some of the boxed lines and masculine features promoted for women.

We clearly want to avoid anything that would identify us with any cult or anti-Christian philosophy; we want to identify with Christ, and in doing so, advertise His hope to this world. The visible demonstration of what we believe is our outward appearance *and* the way we conduct our lives.

Although the principles set forth in the Bible concerning appearance are extremely vital, it is also important to your Christian testimony that you are clean and neat, modest and moderate. As a God-called minister you should carefully avoid wearing anything that is overly expensive or that which calls attention to yourself.

---

[13] Dr. David C. Innes, *Hamilton Square Baptist Church Articles: What Do Your clothes Say About You?*, 1993; online; accessed July 26, 2005; available - http://www.hamiltonsquare.net/articlesClothes.htm.

Conduct, clothing, and style will enhance or detract from the spiritual message you are presenting to others.

Last Minute Checklist

It is good to make sure you are presentable before leaving home. Make a quick mental check from the head to toe.

- ❑ Hair combed
- ❑ Teeth brushed
- ❑ Face washed
- ❑ Cologne or perfume applied (with moderation—some people are allergic)
- ❑ Clothes ironed, clean, and matched
- ❑ Skirt, dress, pants are modest
- ❑ Socks and shoes match, and appropriate for destination
- ❑ Accessories (tie, scarf, etc.) are tasteful and conservative.

4

Ethics Begin at Home

He must manage his own family well,
with children who respect and obey him.
For if a man cannot manage his own household,
how can he take care of God's church?
—1 Timothy 3:4-5 NLT

It is one thing to preach a powerful sermon and project
a perfect image before the congregation on Sunday and
quite another thing to live out the message at home on
Monday. Far too many ministers have fallen prey to the
delusion that as long as the congregation thinks well of me,
I am successful.

The truth is if you fail at home you are disqualified
from fulfilling the leadership role in the church. The first
responsibility of the minister is to manage well his own
house. Paul wrote the biblical requirements for ministerial
leadership to Timothy and asked the parenthetical
question, "If a man does not know how to rule his own

house, how will he take care of the church of God?" Following is the larger context of Paul's instructions.

Biblical Qualifications of a Minister

This is a faithful saying: If a man desires the position of a bishop, he desires a good work.

A bishop then must be *blameless, the husband of one wife, temperate, sober-minded, of good behavior, hospitable, able to teach; not given to wine, not violent, not greedy for money, but gentle, not quarrelsome, not covetous; one who rules his own house well,* having his children in submission with all reverence (for if a man does not know how to rule his own house, how will he take care of the church of God?); *not a novice,* lest being puffed up with pride he fall into the same condemnation as the devil. Moreover he must have *a good testimony among those who are outside,* lest he fall into reproach and the snare of the devil (1 Timothy 3:1-7).

Much of what Paul has to say has little to do with pulpit polish or homiletical excellence. Though these attributes are admirable and important, the only statement Paul made concerning traditional pastoral ministry is that one must be "able to teach." The rest of the passage deals with ethics! As you go through the list of qualifications they can be a little intimidating, nevertheless they are essential elements of ministerial ethics:

"Blameless." He must be above reproach, one of impeccable character, a man with a good reputation. The NLT says, "An elder must be a man whose life cannot be spoken against."

"Husband of one wife." He must be faithful to his wife, a loyal husband. *The Message* says, "committed to his wife." Though some have maintained that this phrase implies the exclusion of any who have previously been married, the sense of most translations suggests it has more to do with fidelity and faithfulness. This may also be understood as the basis for the New Testament doctrine in support of monogamous relationships.

"Temperate." "Sober-minded." "Of good behavior." These characteristics are closely aligned. They describe ethical conduct, self-control, sensible actions, and respectability that lead to a disciplined and moderate lifestyle.

"Hospitable." This is not just tolerating people in your home, but enjoying the company of believers and even strangers in your fellowship.

"Able to teach." Up to this point, each quality had more to do with personal conduct and private disciplines than public ministry. It could be stated in the context that even the "ability to teach" should begin at home!

"Not given to wine." The positive characteristics were given first; now Paul interjects some of the *"nots."* These are labels to avoid. A leader should not be known as one who imbibes. While "a little wine for the stomach's sake" is scriptural, there is less chance of causing another to stumble because of your liberty if you will commit to total abstinence from alcohol.

"Not violent." A leader should not be known as a violent and angry man. There should be no fear in one who approaches you. They should not be intimidated, uncertain as to how you will react. Do your children or your wife fear your angry outbursts? "Let all bitterness, wrath, anger, clamor, and evil speaking be put away from you" (Ephesians 4:31).

"Not greedy for money." A lust for material gain has been the downfall of many ministries. It is not insignificant that Paul adds this notation to the qualifications for a bishop (or pastor).

"Gentle." Let your reputation be one of gentleness. There is nothing wrong with earning the testimony of being a gentle minister. Actually, gentleness is identified with the *fruit of the spirit* and a hallmark quality of the *spirit-filled* life (Galatians 5:22-26).

"Not quarrelsome." While some are always spoiling for a good fight, the minister of the gospel should not have that ambition or reputation. Avoid quarrels. Seek to bring reconciliation and resolution rather than fueling contention and arguments.

"Not covetous." Covetousness is an excessive desire for what another has. In modern culture, it may be a passion for materialism just because someone else has more. Beware of the passion to "keep up with the Joneses."

"One who rules his own house well, having his children in submission with all reverence." The ethical pastor must be a good manager at home. He must have control in his home and have children who respect and obey him. This is not to suggest that the father be a tyrannical, oppressive brute, but rather that he manage the home in

54

such a way as to command respect. Respect that is forced or demanded is not truly respect; it is reluctant obedience with fear of reprisal. True respect is earned and freely given to one who has demonstrated care for those under his charge.

The parenthetical phrase in verse 5 is troubling, "For if a man cannot manage his own household, how can he take care of God's church?" (NLT) Some may ask, "Do I really become disqualified as a minister if my children are not living for God?" If this were true, hundreds of effective ministers that have wayward children would be ineligible to serve as pastors.

It is in the early, formative years of child raising that it is vital to train your child in the principles of Scripture. Teach them while they are young to honor and respect you. Do your part to instill God's truth in their hearts. You cannot slack on your duties as a parent and expect the church to prosper under your leadership. The congregation will judge your ability to lead by how you lead your family. When your child reaches maturity, the choices and decisions he makes are no longer your responsibility. This passage does not forever hold you responsible for other's decisions. It only prompts a parent not to be slothful in parental responsibilities.

"Not a novice." Those who are called of God should exercise their ministry to gain experience, study to develop understanding, and seek wisdom from above to more effectively relate to those to whom they will minister. James said, "If any of you lacks wisdom, let him ask of God, who gives to all liberally and without reproach, and it will be given to him" (James 1:5).

"_Having a good testimony among those who are outside._" A minister must be concerned about what others think of him. A good reputation is the greatest asset a minister can possess. Always, in his mind, he must ask the question, "How will this look to others? Will this bring a bad name against me or against the church?" Paul is saying, "Timothy, be especially concerned about how things appear to unbelievers, those who are outside."

> A good reputation is the greatest asset a minister can possess.

In the final verses, two other phrases to note are the "lest" phrases (vs. 6, 7). The term contrasts the failure in one area revealing the consequences in another area. It is the antithesis, the counter balance of results.

Paul insists that the pastor should not be a new convert (a novice), "_lest being puffed up with pride he fall into the same condemnation as the devil._" If a new believer has not had time to mature in his faith, he is more vulnerable to pride or conceit. The end result could be the damnation of his soul. Lucifer's pride got him evicted from heaven! Paul adds this somber warning following the admonition to be a mature believer before accepting the role of pastor.

The other phrase suggests that a pastor must have a _good testimony_ among unbelievers "_lest he fall into reproach and the snare of the devil._" Satan has set a trap for every God-called man or woman. It is his ploy to cause failure in the ministry and ruin the good reputation of the person and the church. This trap may be moral failure, financial misconduct, personal indiscretion, material indulgence, or willful pride. Any black mark of blame that the enemy of your soul can attach to your character will be attempted. Guard your character with tenacious purpose.

Priorities in Christian Living

Having established the biblical qualifications for ministry (essentially pastors) there are some basic priorities that should here be established. In the effort to be a good and godly minister of the gospel, there are times when choices must be made between equally essential needs in areas of ministry. It doesn't take long in the ministry to realize that you cannot be everything to everyone. You must choose how to invest your time and how to expend your energy in ministry. For this reason, it is imperative that there be a clear distinction between the demands on your ministry. What is most important? What do I say yes to, and to what can I say no?

Charles Grisham, in a book chapter entitled *The Minister and His Family*, stated that the proper priorities of ministry ought to be in this order,[14]

1. Ministry to the Lord
2. Ministry to the family
3. Ministry to the church
4. Ministry to those outside the church

---

[14] Charles Grisham, "The Minister and His Family," in *The Pentecostal Minister*, edited by J.L. Hall and David K. Bernard (Hazelwood, MO: Word Aflame Press, 1991), 49.

The following chart illustrates this hierarchy of priorities:

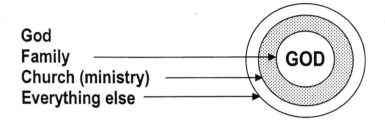

God
Family
Church (ministry)
Everything else

GOD

1. God

With God at the center, everything else comes into focus, into proper orbit. Priorities are maintained as long as God is at the center and occupies the place of supremacy in your life.

Much will be written about the other orbs of life and ministry, but this is the heart and the most vital part. Seek to know God and keep him in the place of primary priority.

> But *seek first the kingdom of God and His righteousness,* and all these things shall be added to you (Matthew 6:33).

As a minister of the gospel, it is easy to confuse *ministry* and *God.* We often think of doing ministry as serving God. If I'm preaching about Jesus, praying for people in Jesus' name, and witnessing about His love to an unbeliever, isn't that serving God? It is possible to become so busy doing things *for* Him that we neglect spending time *with* Him! God must be returned to the center.

If we confuse our ministry and our relationship with God, our family will suffer. If our relationship *with* God is inextricably tied to our ministry *for* God, then we are never able to put our family before church. To say "no" to someone who wants to spend the evening unburdening their heart, so you can spend one evening with your family, somehow becomes a rejection of God. Family priorities then get pushed to number three, and all our activity in ministry takes precedence over the needs of those closest to us.

Keeping God in the center and maintaining our relationship with Him in devotional time, prayer, and worship, keeps the order clear. If our relationship with God is right, it will be easier to maintain a right relationship with our family. If these two relationships are in order, then we will be more effective in the time we spend in ministry to the needs of others. Further, the concentric circles of relationships continue to develop in their proper sphere.

2. Family

No one knows like your family if you are a true Christian or not. These are the people that see you when you are up and when you are down. They are the ones that witness your disappointments and failures. We all have weak moments; at times we fail. However, these are not indications of hopelessness; they are the evidence of humanity. We are individuals with corruptible natures who need the heavenly Father on a daily basis to be what we should be.

To be a Christian in front of the family is not asking for perfection. It is just a reminder to your loved ones that, "when I fall, I get up ... so you can, too." It is a gentle "I love you," when someone else makes a mistake. It is a sincere "I'm sorry," when you are wrong. It is *living-out* the overcoming Christian life on a daily basis in front of your family, with all its ugly mistakes and beautiful forgiveness.

No one is perfect, so we cannot expect perfection from our family. Your children will disappoint you; your wife will fall short of your expectations. Wives, your husband will not be able to meet all your needs. In other words, you can expect failure in life. Even Christian families experience disappointments and unfulfilled expectations. In those times of bitter disappointment, look to Jesus for his strength and experience the grace of God in restoration.

As a spiritual leader, whether you are a man or a woman, your family will look to you for spiritual guidance in their lives. Men, you are to lead by example, by instruction, and by following Christ yourself. Women, you also have a responsibility for spiritual leadership; seek God, pray for your family, and teach your children to love God.

Being a minister and a husband is not all teaching and preaching. Relax with your family. Have fun together. The memories you make laughing and enjoying each other will last for a lifetime. Your family will see you under pressure, they will see you in the pulpit declaring the Word of God, but when they see you laugh, they see you as a real person. When you can play on the floor with your children, they see you as one that steps out of the leadership world into their world—the real world.

3. Church

Next in the circles of priority is ministry to the church. To the pastor or minister, this is a very important aspect of his life. Men find significance by the work that they do and the service they perform. When men meet, one of the first questions they ask is, "What do you do?" They immediately want to know what another does for a living. It is more than casual conversation. There is an assessment of an individual's worth by the work that he does. If he says, "Oh, I stay at home with the kids; my wife works," the value of the man drops several notches! While women may experience this bias from other women, men are much more sensitive to the significance of their job.

The conscientious minister thrives on the service he performs for the congregation. When someone comments on the service, it is a commendation or a reflection on the self-worth of the minister. If someone is blessed by the sermon the minister feels validated. If someone complains about the length of the message and the conviction from the Word preached, the minister may feel that he has failed in his task. Charles Grisham said, "The man of God needs the support, strength, and understanding of his family as he carries the burden of the flock of God and continues to lead his own household."[15]

When things do not go well at home, a minister *must not* take his frustrations to church with him and conversely, he should not take the church problems home.

---

[15] Grisham, 50-51.

This is a most difficult requirement. A carpenter can pack his tools, call it a day, and forget his job until the next day, but a minister can never leave his calling. He must always be a minister and aware of his responsibilities. He cannot quit caring for a hurting believer just because it is 5:00 PM. He cannot forget the early morning surgery, the late night call for prayer, the family with a failing marriage, and the man who waits for a visit in his jail cell.

Since the role of the minister is 24/7, it is easy to unload that burden at home. The listening ear of a wife can share the difficulties of the day, but there must be some time when you talk of something else and take time to listen. Your wife may also need a listening ear with which to share the details of her day. Children need to be able to share their concerns as well. Talk about plans for the future (other than the church). Plan a family vacation. Talk about current events. Discuss political issues. Paint a room or work on the car. Mow the yard and trim the hedges.

When you are at church and involved in other people's lives, give them your attention and support. Forget your problems and attend to theirs. If you are upset with the dog, there is no need to take it out on those who come to midweek Bible study! These people are tired from a long day's work. They have made the effort to be in church. They deserve your best!

4. Everything Else

All other demands on the minister must find time in the last orb of priority. There is only so much time for anything in life. If it is not important enough to be placed in the first three spheres it should not receive any higher priority in your schedule.

At Home with your Spouse

If you want to know the status of a Christian, just ask his or her spouse. Children in the home can also give you some great insight, and if around the age of five, happily reveal all the family secrets! The appearance a ministry couple represents to the public should be a reflection of the life they lead at home. The badge of behavior a man shows in public is an icon of the way he treats his wife in private. A congregation should be able to feel the same warmth, care, and attentiveness the minister shows his wife in public.

Paul wrote about these important areas of relationships in the Book of Ephesians, and made the parallel of our familial relationships as reflecting the spiritual relationships that God ordained between Christ and the church,

Submitting to one another in the fear of God. *Wives, submit to your own husbands, as to the Lord.* For the husband is head of the wife, as also Christ is head of the church; and He is the Savior of the body. Therefore, just as the church is subject to Christ, so let the wives be to their own husbands in everything.

Husbands, love your wives, just as Christ also loved the church and gave Himself for her, ... So husbands ought to love their own wives as their own bodies; _he who loves his wife loves himself._ For no one ever hated his own flesh, but nourishes and cherishes it, just as the Lord does the church. ...

This is a great mystery, but I speak concerning Christ and the church. Nevertheless _let each one of you in particular so love his own wife as himself, and let the wife see that she respects her husband_ (Ephesians 5:21-33).

Without going into an extensive study of this passage let us simply say the lesson summarizes this: each person is to reciprocate the spirit of Christ toward the other in marriage. Love, respect, honor, obedience and compassion are all virtues created in Heaven and should be present in the holy union of marriage. The husband is commanded to love his wife; the wife is commanded to submit to or respect her husband.

When you love someone, you do not intentionally want to hurt them. Hurting each other physically is out of the question. Many couples would not think of battering each other in an outburst of rage and causing physical pain; yet emotional battering seems to be a free-for-all today.[16]

Because of anger, couples spit out unkind words, withhold themselves sexually, or close up, refusing to talk at all. This may accelerate to expressing hurtful comebacks in public. God is not pleased when we intentionally hurt

---

[16] If you have resorted to physical attacks, please get help immediately. Seek the intervention and aid of a caring minister or Christian counselor.

each other. The bruise an outburst of harsh words causes to a heart may essentially do more damage than a *black eye*.

Degrading your spouse in public is not an expression of respect or honor. It is the opposite and causes disgrace, not only to the spouse and all those present, but to you as a minister; it degrades the very Christ you represent. Recall how uncomfortable you are when someone begins tearing down another in your presence. Never allow this to creep into your marriage.

Even joking, chiding remarks in public are hurtful. The public arena is not a place to air disagreements or other less desirable traits in your mate. We should be caring enough to approach a touchy subject in private. If there is something your spouse does that annoys you, approach the subject in private, rather than jokingly dragging it out like dirty laundry while a crowd of friends look on.

When in the pulpit ministering to others, lighthearted teasing sometimes makes the audience feel they know you and your spouse better. It can be a tool of expressing love in public without being mushy. But any comments about your spouse, or to your spouse, from the pulpit should be kept to *lighthearted* comments. In other words, *light* meaning not-heavy or so personal as to bring shameful embarrassment, and *hearted* to mean it comes from the soft side of the heart, not the hard side. Teasing in public should never reveal a rift between the couple. If it makes the audience feel uncomfortable, that is a clue it is in bad taste. If it is hurtful to your spouse, and he/she expresses this, apologize right away and re-evaluate your comments for the future.

I enjoy seeing couples in leadership positions act like they are in love. This does not require an embarrassing display of public affection, but it does call for some tender moments of expression that are perfectly acceptable in public. Such as, holding hands, an arm around one another, or a pat on the arm or back are ways of showing affection without too much embarrassment.

The Unsaved or Backslidden Spouse

You may not have the blessing of a spouse living for God. Sometimes you may feel lonely even though you are married because you cannot share the most exciting, closest things to your heart with your mate. Feel confident that God knew when He called you that you would be in this situation today. He knows when your spouse will surrender to His call. You cannot make your husband or wife live for God. No one can make them. God won't even *make* them live for Him. They have to make the decision alone, when they are ready. You must keep looking to God for your strength. Don't guilt yourself into believing that you have failed because you have not caused them to want to live for God. Your responsibility is to be a good husband or wife to your unsaved spouse; be the *best* you can be.

In your situation it would be easy to covet other couples' relationships. It is not wise to look at other couples and wish you had a wife like that or that you married a man with that dedication. You don't want discontent to settle in your heart. Satan can disillusion you with pipe dreams that are nothing more than bait to cause problems in your marriage. Be content with the spouse

God gave you and trust Him to work out the difficulty an unsaved spouse causes in your ministry. Be wise in your dreams and wishes. As you work through life with God's wisdom, He works through you to draw your spouse unto Him.

The fruit of the righteous is a tree of life, and *he who wins souls is wise* (Proverbs 11:30).

The following are some guidelines to observe in your relationship with an unsaved spouse:

- Don't be ashamed of your unsaved spouse. Make him/her feel welcome to come to any church function you are involved in.

- Include him/her in your dreams and ambitions.

- If you are a woman in ministry and your husband is unsaved, still seek his counsel and value his opinion.

- Submit to your spouse, according to the biblical instruction.

- Stay true to your vows and let your spouse know that you intend to love him/her and be faithful forever.

- Love, love, love, love! And then when you are done, love some more. You cannot love your unsaved spouse too much. Showing love unconditionally is showing them God—for God is love.

A Word to the Husband

A ministry can be _made_ or _messed-up_ by the wife you choose. The most crucial decision you will make, after your commitment to God, is who you will marry. I've seen many men hampered by unwilling wives. I have seen others who wouldn't be worth dirt without their wives!

You must be secure in your call and then seek someone who will share your call. You have been called; your spouse may not have been. Your call may be specific; your spouse may have a general call and feel your specifics are just your preference. It takes more grace for a spouse to follow your call.

> It takes more grace for a spouse to follow your call.

District Boards that interview ministerial candidates are more concerned about the wife (_or husband, as the case may be_) of the team than ever before. Most boards require the spouse to appear with the applicant. It is a team effort! The Bible states that the two become one flesh.

And Adam said: "This _is_ now bone of my bones And flesh of my flesh; She shall be called Woman, Because she was taken out of Man. Therefore a man shall leave his father and mother and be joined to his wife, and _they shall become one flesh_ (Genesis 2:23-24).

A Wife is a *"Helper"*

And the LORD God said, *"It is* not good that man should be alone; I will make him a *helper comparable* to him."* So Adam gave names to all cattle, to the birds of the air, and to every beast of the field. But for Adam there was not found a *helper comparable* to him (Genesis 2:18, 20).

A *"help meet"* in the KJV is identified in other translations as:

- "a helper comparable" - NKJV
- "a helper as his partner" - NRSV
- "a helper suitable for him" - NASB, NIV
- "a helper who is right for him" - NCV

The Hebrew word for *help meet* is *"ezer"* (עֵזֶר). Its meaning suggests that she will supply what is missing. He is *incomplete* without her. *She supplies what he is lacking!*

The Hebrew word *"ezer"* usually refers to God being our helper. He is our supply, our help. Every married man should see his companion as a value to the ministry. Recognize that your spouse also has a ministry.

> It is essential that the husband and wife be united in the call of God.

It is essential that the husband and wife be united in the call of God. It is impossible to separate a man and wife when considering the call of God.

Her Needs

1. Security
2. Intimate conversation
3. Sincere appreciation
4. Affection
5. Affirmation

When these ingredients are present, the wife feels fulfilled. Early in a woman's life, she begins to search for someone to love and take care of her—someone who appreciates her and values her. Once she has found the "one and only" the search is over, but the need for love and affirmation is continual. As a lush houseplant thrives on weekly watering, she needs to hear that she is loved; she needs to be affirmed, valued, and cherished continually to be replenished. She will not search for it elsewhere if she receives it from the one she has given her heart to. It is the husband's golden opportunity to be a true knight in shining armor to his wife on a daily basis by simply loving, cherishing and affirming her.

A woman feels valued when she is shown affection outside the marriage bed. A well-known, respected minister once said that a kiss is not a kiss unless it is more than five seconds. A kiss to a woman is more than foreplay. Even after twenty-plus years of marriage, a woman feels cheap and used if her only recognizable talent is how good she is in bed. She needs to be appreciated for her mind, her humor, and her effort to maintain a smooth household and raise happy children.

A Word to the Wife

A woman holds the key to the success or failure of her minister husband. I'm sure you have heard it said that "behind every successful man is a good woman." A supportive wife helps her husband beat the odds in the midst of financial difficulties, church problems, discouragement, and the temptation to give up altogether and quit. Her attitude toward the ministry reveals to others how she feels about the closest "man of God" in her life—her husband. Therefore it is almost impossible for him to achieve success if she has a negative concept of his ministry. However, if he feels her support, the whole world could be against him and yet he will persevere.

I have heard evangelists' wives publicly voice their displeasure of traveling from church to church conducting revivals. One complained about not having a place of her own. Another fussed about home-schooling the children, eating out all the time, and being away from her parents. They had lost the adventure; the fulfillment. They no longer see the need for their ministry. Eventually, the evangelist may give in to discouragement and resign from the evangelistic field, seeking to please a discontented wife.

If the wife decides she does not want to be a part of her husband's ministry, it almost always ends in defeat. To forsake his ministry in an effort to save his marriage is no better than forfeiting his marriage to preserve his ministry. This difficult ethical dilemma can be avoided if his wife will find reconciliation in her own life between her desires and the calling of God. If together, they will surrender to the will of the Lord they will find God's peace and strength in yielding to His will.

His Needs

Men have different needs than women, but they are needs just the same. When you desire to make your husband happy, you will search for ways to please him. Among other more practical things, men need to feel appreciated, respected, and admired.

Men need to know that they are appreciated as the provider. A man needs to hear that his hard work is valued. Every penny he provides for shopping, fun spending, or bills, is hard earned. He should hear how much you appreciate his efforts to support his family.

If you are in ministry, and your husband is not, it is still important to seek his counsel and approval on your decisions. You come under his authority and when you have his blessing on your ministry, there is no limit to what God can do through both of you. You are a team. Showing your husband that you respect his opinions and guidance shows him that you trust his relationship with God, whether he ever gets behind a pulpit or not.

Do you remember how you looked at your husband before you were married? You may have gazed into his eyes and thought, "He is the most handsome man I've ever seen." He felt the admiration come from your heart. Marriages are built upon mutual respect and affirmation. Every day, relive the awe and adoration you felt in your courtship. Keeping a marriage alive depends on both of you. A woman who admires her husband is an irresistible, godly woman. When his needs are met, a husband will do just about anything to please his wife.

Practical Needs

It is amazing how some practical deeds on the wife's part can fulfill a husband. When a man comes home to a neat, well kept home, it shows that you appreciate the house he has provided for you. He needs to feel that he is successful in his responsibility to support and take care of his family. When you take care of the things he gives you and maintain them, it shows that you value the gift, whether it is a house plant or a home to live in. When you cook a delicious meal with the groceries he has provided, it gives him a sense of accomplishment similar to your feelings while creating it.

Keep his children neat and clean. Your husband can see your pride and attentiveness in the children he gave you. When you nurture his children, it is an extension of his physical needs you are attending to.

A man needs a job. It helps him feel that he is worth something. If he cannot see his ministry as a job, he will not feel fulfilled. He needs to be encouraged to keep regular hours when he is a full-time minister, but not made to feel guilty for relaxing, when the opportunity comes to take a break.

A man also has sexual needs. These physical needs must be fulfilled by his wife to nurture an intimate relationship with him. He thrives on sexual satisfaction as the wife thrives on affection. When these needs are met in both spouses they each experience a sense of intimate bonding.

Male Ego

God placed within a man the desire to be the provider. This feeds that *male ego* that puzzles most women. When the male ego is nurtured, the man rises to a new level of attentive behavior. If a woman could see the

concept of the power of feeding her husband's ego, she would also see that the results reciprocate dividends beyond her expectations. This is not about *sending him off* on an ego trip that takes him away from her. It is exactly the opposite. It is tapping in to his needs as a husband. Find out what builds up his self-esteem, and bless him with compliments and affirmation. Men want to hear that they are doing a good job at whatever they are trying to achieve. Once they feel that ego start to inflate with sincere positive actions, they can't show enough affection to the person providing it.

Check Your Love Level

As a couple, it is good to check your love level with each other frequently. A busy schedule can rob you of the most beautiful relationship God has ordained. Marriage is the most precious relationship because it is compared to the heavenly relationship of Christ and His bride. Take a few moments each day to make sure your level of love is at its highest level with your spouse.

- Affirm each other by saying "I love you" at least twice a day, once in the morning and once before bedtime.

- Kiss passionately with no sexual intentions at least once a day (preferably early and it should last five seconds or more).

- Allow your children to see you show love toward each other. Holding hands, hugging each other, or just saying "I love you" in front of them, are wonderful examples of true love.

- Show others your love for each other in an acceptable expression of affection in public.

- Never go to bed angry.

At Home with Your Children

Love your children, discipline them, and spend time with them. They are an eternal investment. Your children are your most valuable asset. The Bible says when we have children, it is a reward (Psalm 127:3). The present world-view that children are a liability is directly contrary to God's view and value of children. Today children are seen as a nuisance to one pursuing a career, and held in such low esteem that abortion is on the rise and in many places a legal choice. Large cities like San Francisco and New York are now concerned with the lack of children in their inner city communities. An article in the Associated Press stated the concern that we are at a crossroads, "... moving toward a place where we could have an infrastructure of children's services and no children."[17] It's no wonder, when all we hear is how inconvenient it is to be saddled with little ones. We must be careful not to bend an ear to what the world is saying, and be reminded what God says about our children.

The Bible not only calls children a heritage and a reward, but it encourages us to have a "quiver full," which some say is about five. It also tells us that we can actually be happy about having that many children!

> Behold, *children are a heritage from the LORD*, the *fruit of the womb is a reward*. Like arrows in the hand of a warrior, so are the children of one's youth. *Happy is the man who has his quiver full of them* (Psalm 127:3-5a).

We cannot take our beautiful home, nice car or other valuable assets with us when we die, but there is something of great value we will be allowed to carry into eternity—the children with which God has rewarded us. If we take time to carefully raise them in the admonition of the Lord, they are the only asset we can take into eternity with us. They are our most valuable possessions. Many times we must be reminded of their value especially when they get under our feet, scream and run through the house, or cling to our dress hem. When our teenager slams the bedroom door in an effort to "just be alone," we must lift

---

[17] Lisa Leff, *Where Have All The Children Gone:* Associated Press online, accessed May 24, 2005; available from http://pqasb.pqarchiver.com/ap.

our eyes heavenward and say, "Lord, this is still a good reward," and mean it.

Children need to hear you pray. If they don't hear you pray, how do they know you do it? They will learn how to approach the throne of God by your example. Teach them to pray at a young age. Take them to the prayer room with you at church, and train them to respect this time of talking to the King of kings. Show them how to worship in church. Be an example in worship.

Children need to see you apologize when you have offended your spouse. It is not good for them to see you fight, but it is impossible for them to be sheltered from an occasional disagreement. They need to see how you work it out. When you do it right, they take notes in their little minds and try it on their friends.

In the busyness of the life of a minister, children often times are overlooked and set aside. A pastor will feel guilty taking time out to play with the kids or go someplace fun. His times of leisure are few and far between. Time flies. Before you know it, you wonder who that young man walking through the door is. Just yesterday he was a toddler pulling on your leg. Or, who is that beautiful young lady receiving her high school diploma *or* getting married? Just yesterday she was pretending to be a mommy, holding a doll in her arms. Make the most of the time you have with your children. Children not only need you to *pray* with them, but they need you to *play* with them also.

Our families must have high priority in what we value. God entrusted children to us as our first mission field. They are the wards He entrusted us with to try out our faith. If we reach out to the community and overlook our children, we are missing the rare opportunity to win a soul that God has literally placed in our laps.

Discipline Your Children

To approach the subject of discipline, the subject of physical abuse is always lurking in the wings, ready to pour out guilt and discourage parents from the needful application of correction. When you understand the difference between discipline and abuse, it helps to divide the two into proper perspective.

Discipline, by definition, is teaching self-control, training by instruction and practice. It is teaching someone to obey and accept the authority setting the rules. The most physical application of discipline is to use punishment to gain control or enforce obedience. See how this differs from abuse.

> Discipline is teaching, training, and using positive principles as motivation.

Abuse is to misuse someone wrongly and improperly, hurting or injuring them by mistreatment. It is to rape, molest or force sexual activity upon someone. To assault someone with contemptuous, coarse words that are insulting and berating is considered to be verbal abuse.

Discipline is used to build character. Abuse is used to tear it down. Discipline is teaching, training, and using positive principles as motivation. Abuse is coercing, demanding, and using fear as a motive. These two approaches to behavior modification are opposite. When discipline becomes destructive and harmful it no longer produces the intended result but digresses into abuse.

There are many ways to abuse a child without breaking the law. Once I saw a parent squeeze a child's collar bone until he brought the child to his knees in tears. The parent left no bruises, but it was very painful and embarrassing to the child. God never intended for us to humiliate our children or to hurt them beyond repair, but children left to themselves spell trouble. When we study the difference between the two, we see that the biblical call for correcting children does not fall under the harsh, unreasonable actions of abuse. God expects us to point our children in the right direction, even if it takes a little persuasion, but never does the Word imply that it should be harmful to the child.

Balance is a great buffer in every part of our lives. It once again helps parents gauge the course of action needed in training their children. Fear of someone turning them over to the authorities has put a damper on many young parents correcting their children in public. Thus they have lost complete control over their children. The same people who glare at them for correcting a rather well-behaved child in public are the same ones that glare at those who will not take their child in hand when they are being disruptive. You cannot gauge your disciplinary actions by what others think. Yes, you must be careful to minimize corporal punishment such as spanking in public, but if you do your homework the task in public is much more effective. We started teaching our children at a very young age to sit on the couch during prayer time. When it came time to go to church, they knew what to do while everyone else was praying. It also taught them that there is a time to run and play and a time to sit quietly and color.

Proverbs 22:6 says, "Train up a child in the way he should go, And when he is old he will not depart from it." We have a promise. When we do our part, the natural outgrowth is rewarding. Someone said "in the way he should go" means to nurture the child in the way he is bent. In other words, find his gift and train him up to go in the way he is bent, and it will be easy for him to keep to the path. If we encourage our children to do things they are good at, it gives them confidence to excel. Nothing is more motivating than success and the same rule applies in raising children. Give them every opportunity to be successful and they will bloom and grow like a carefully nurtured rose garden. We plant, we water, we prune; and then we leave the growing up to God.

> **Nothing is more motivating than success and the same rule applies in raising children.**

God, our heavenly Father, is the perfect example of parenthood. He loved us enough to die for us, yet His balance is chastisement when we need discipline. His perfect example of balance between love and discipline is one we should examine closely and use on our children. Children need guidelines. They need the secure enclosure of rules and restrictions.

80

When you set the rules, there need to be consequences if the rules are broken. The rules need to be clear and understood as well as the consequences. One without the other leads to unfairness and frustration, not only on the part of the parent but on the child also.

Frustration can escalate into anger, which is not good. Anger-induced discipline is dangerous. Anger has a way of clouding your sense of judgment. If you are angry, it is best to wait until you have cooled off before confronting a child who has broken the rules. You can think better and judge the situation with much more wisdom.

Anger is a poor motivator for children. In fact, if you find that your child is tuning you out, re-evaluate your voice control. If a child constantly hears a parent yell, he will eventually tune it out. A parent that requires action with a command is much more successful and does not have to yell or scream to achieve the desired response from the child. It takes some follow-through discipline on your part, but it is a much more peaceful technique. Remember during discipline to be calm, be cool, and be fair.

Children that seem to *forget* how to behave may respond to creative discipline. Tailor the discipline to match the infraction. For example, when our little girl wrote on her doll's face with a permanent marker, we took all her writing tools away for a designated length of time. It was very traumatic for her. She loved to write, especially in church. She was miserable when the length of the punishment went over a Sunday. Even though she was only three years old, she had to tell her Sunday school teacher why she was not allowed to write in church. While the other children were coloring and drawing, our daughter had to sit and watch. For this particular infraction, the prolonged prohibition of no crayons, pencils, or markers was something that she remembered for a long time.

On the other hand, permissiveness is also damaging to children. Children gauge your love by the limits placed on them. Parents who love their children will go to extreme measures to teach them not to play in traffic. Why? Because they don't want their children to run into the street and get hit by a car or even killed. Children interpret apathetic attitudes toward disciplines as a lack of love and care for them.

The best policy when trying to discipline your children is to find a balance. Think about the porridge in the story of Goldilocks and the three bears. Discipline should not be *too hard* or *too soft*, but it should be administered *just right* to be most effective.

Give Your Time

All those projects at the church will wait. They will be there after you have spent the valuable time you need with your family. Your children need a mommy and daddy first. Don't feel guilty saying, "I'm sorry, that is our family night," or "Thank you for the invitation, but I have reserved that time to be with my son" or "my daughter."

You will never regret the quality time you spend with your children. You may not have an entire day you can devote to them on a consistent basis, but the time you set aside for them will reap dividends that all the money in the world cannot buy. The busier you are, the more valuable your time with your children will be. They know when you are busy, and they will analyze their importance to you by the time you sacrifice for them. Your children's self-acceptance is affected by the value you place on their company.

Sometimes younger children misbehave because they want attention—any kind of attention. If you will give them the attention they need, they will not try to attract your attention with bad behavior. I do not agree with the old adage, "Children are to be seen and not heard." If children are not heard, they will do something to be heard. If older children are not heard, they will find an ear that will hear them. God forbid that the needed ear is someone that will lead them away from the precious truth of God's Word.

> **Our children have been given to us as a heritage from the Lord.**

Sometimes older kids wander from the truth not because of rebellion, but because of a need to be included, which they unfortunately don't find at home. If the church members come first, the children may feel that they come second, and only after the needs of the church are met, will their needs be met.

Our children have been given to us as a heritage from the Lord. God gave them to us to pass down the blessing of salvation, the knowledge of truth, and the love of God to their children (our grandchildren), and to all those who come after us.

Children should be treated with respect, just like an adult. If a child is accustomed to being treated with respect, he will learn how to treat others the same way.

Approve, Support, and Compliment

When children are young, parents are the most important people in their lives. They need your approval, support, and public recognition. A balance of praise and instruction is most effective for perceptive learning. A child will even understand that the pain of correction is necessary when it is mixed with loving praise. Children need to know that whatever they do, whether right or wrong, they have your approval as a person. When they do something right, watch their faces light up after a word of praise. Even when they do something wrong, a reassuring word will help remind them that your love and acceptance is not based on their performance. Your approval is of supreme importance to them.

Your children need your support. Heaven knows they get pressure from the congregation. Without anyone saying anything, they feel pressure just being preacher's kids. They may not hear it from you, but someone is expecting them to be an example to the other children. After all, they are preacher's kids. If you reassure them that you don't expect them to be perfect, they will be better able to deal with the other pressures. They need to know that it is all right to be normal, and normal kids make mistakes.

Children need to know when they make you proud. If you have a chance to compliment them in public, they may appear a little embarrassed at first, but knowing they have made you a proud parent is worth a few seconds of embarrassment. Older children are more easily embarrassed in public, but they still need to be affirmed. A card or note commending them on a job well done is more subtle, and yet you are still reminding them you are proud they are part of the family and that they are special to you. Cards should not take the place of verbal affirmation. Good kids need to hear that they are good.

Teach Respect

Showing respect is rapidly becoming a lost art in our world. I have heard well-meaning believers complain about preachers' children lacking respectful attitudes toward other adults. (This is not to say that members' children don't have the same problem.) It is never acceptable for children to treat adults with disrespect. Most parents want their children to be liked and accepted. Disrespect among preachers' kids may not be the result of faulty teaching. Simply failing to notice may be the culprit. Paying attention to how your children treat others may produce a great revelation. Encourage your children to answer in a respectful way, even if they disagree.

Children need to be respected by their parents. Many children were not even wanted at birth, let alone respected. When children feel no respect, the base to build reciprocation of respect is gone. In other words, treat your children with respect in order to teach your children to respect. You are the example that will be their pattern. How long has it been since you heard a child say, "Yes, ma'am; no, sir; thank you; or please?" These words are not just a string of old-fashioned jargon. Learning to voice words that show respect is a valuable tool toward exercising respect for others.

Remind your child that he is special because he is God's child, not because he is a preacher's child. If he has the concept that he is on the same level as the church members' children, it will remove much of the pressure he may feel from critical members. It will also nip a prideful, superior attitude in an extroverted, over-confident child.[18]

Be a Shelter

There may be times when it is very difficult to hide church problems from your children. They will sense an undercurrent of dissension, without a word being spoken. If you uphold the members of the congregation in their eyes, there will probably never be a justifiable need for your children to become bitter or angry at the people you minister to.

Many preachers lose their young teenagers because of unfair small talk against the believers. It breeds a spirit of gossip, dissension, and disunity in a child that sprouts rebellion in the teen years. Do you wonder where that rebellion came from? It was born out of all the garbage and trash that was planted in his or her heart as a child. You will do your child the best service possible by sheltering him from anything that would cripple his faith in the people of God. Just as you would shelter church members from trouble, your children should also be spared the worry of church problems.

---

[18] Gayla M. Baughman, *Christian Social Graces: A Guide for the Pentecostal Woman*, (Pleasanton: Baughman Group, 2001), 361-366.

Unsaved Children

The subject of backslidden children came up in one of our ethics classes. Does this affect the minister's ability to pastor? How does it affect the congregation? Is it more critical to your ministry if the child is younger when he strays from the truth than when he is an adult? The answers to these questions may seem ambiguous, not because there is no answer, but because every family, every church, and every child is different.

There are children who "try their wings" in their teen years. In some cases, because of the love and understanding of a sensitive congregation directed toward that young person, they quickly find their way back home. We all pray for people like that in our congregations. On the other hand, if the child has encountered even one critical, embittered saint that kicks him while he is down, it may take years for him to recover. Each child is different. You raise them relatively the same way, teaching them the best you know how to love God. One may be bent toward the direction of the world while the other bends toward God. One may be rebellious, and the other dedicated to God in an extraordinary way. The background, home environment, and godly teaching you give each child come from the same source, and yet many times they make very different choices.

Remember the parable of the seed and the sower? (See Matthew 13.) Think of yourself as the sower, the planter of the seed. You sow seeds of truth on the earthen hearts of your children. The seed is good; there is nothing wrong with the seed. You, the sower, have done your job well; it is the condition of the ground that makes all the difference. It depends on the condition of everyone's heart, how truth takes hold. Some children are soft earth. The seed _takes_ from the beginning and springs forth into abundant life. Others need time. The ground is hard and unwilling to accept the seed. The ground must be tilled, stones must be removed and weeds constantly uprooted. Finally, after the sower has planted seeds time and time again, going back to painful conditioning, the seed takes root.

Your children must be reminded that God loves them. Pull up the weeds of doubt and let them know that God does not give up easily. Cast out the stones of anger and bitterness they have harbored and replace them with your own love and patience. Do not give up. Keep sowing the seed, continue loving your children. One day, their hearts will be ready and the seed will take root.

> They cannot go to heaven on your faith. It must become their own.

Many parents blame themselves for their children wandering away from God. It is not your fault that your children stray away. God gave them a choice. Your desire is that they choose to live for God. Sometimes it takes time for children to realize that they do indeed have a choice and given that liberty sends them on a journey searching for truth.

You cannot make the choice for them. They cannot go to heaven on your faith. It must become their own. The story of the prodigal son is a great comfort to many parents that find themselves in the place of the father (Luke 15:11-31). He could not go with the son who wanted to explore the world, he had obligations at home. You have obligations to your church and ministry. You cannot go with your children while they search for their own faith. The father of the prodigal did what he could. He waited, looking down the path, expecting his son to come home every day. You cannot shove truth and faith down your backslidden child's throat, but you can wait, and continue to look down the path with anticipation for his return. Keep watching, and waiting, one day you will see him coming around the bend, finally coming home.

The idea *an ounce of prevention is worth a pound of cure* may be one answer to your part in this heart wrenching drama. If you portray your children as normal, not always perfect, and sometimes even a little mischievous, as are the saints' kids, it puts them on the same level. Thus, the congregation is exposed to a child like theirs. This does not exclude the isolated case of a jealous saint that lashes out at or about your family. In that case, there is nothing you can do about the saint, but you can teach your children that their performance is not based on or judged by others.

It may seem the impact on a minister is not as crucial if his children choose to backslide after they are out on their own, unless, of course, they attend his church. In which case, it can be very devastating to the entire congregation. A consistent, loving father will do everything within his power to save a drowning child. The same is true with spiritual drowning. This is probably the natural response from a parent. The results are complicated with the fact that you are not only responsible for your children, but for a congregation that looks to you as an example and for direction.

Preachers' Kids

Being a PK (preacher's kid) should be projected as a privilege, not a pain. If you think it is a privilege, your children will likely think so, too. Fall in love with the ministry and they will, too.

Minimize the pressure on your children. There is enough pressure on youth today without the added pressure of being in the fishbowl of the minister's home. Others can make mistakes, and they go  unnoticed. When the PK makes a mistake, it seems that everyone knows it. Do your best to prevent unreasonable expectations from adding to the burden of growing up. Let your response to failures be an illustration of the heavenly Father's response of grace and forgiveness.

Try to be fair in every respect. Don't expect too much or too little. In an effort to be the showcase of a perfect pastor's home, a parent may be tempted to be hard and unbending in the rules established for the home. On the other hand, it is possible to be too slack and undisciplined, suggesting that the pastor's children are not expected to live under the same guidelines preached over the pulpit.

90

Whatever you preach for other families will be expected in your family. You cannot make exceptions for your children and be hard-line in your requirements for someone else. That is not to suggest that you neglect to preach convictions and standards in the church. That doesn't mean that your children will not struggle with some of the convictions that you hold and proclaim. It does mean that you should treat your own children with mercy in the same way you treat another young person in the church. If you remove a church member's kid from the choir for immorality, you will be expected to do the same to your child.

One of the biggest areas of complaint in ministry will be the perceived inequity in your decisions concerning church families and your own family. You can never satisfy everyone. Some will think that you are too hard on your children, while another will think that you are too lax. The blessed middle ground of moderation must be sought and defended. It is your child and your responsibility as a parent to do the right thing for him, regardless of the pressure of a parishioner's opinion.

Advantages of a PK Home

Preacher's kids have great advantages over other children who are not raised in a minister's home.

- They have the opportunity to travel to conferences, regional and district meetings, camp meetings, and sometimes other countries.

- They get to meet other young people. Their circle of friends tends to be much broader, as they develop relationships in their travels.

- They have leadership opportunities, as other youth naturally look to the PK for peer leadership.

- They have an inside track in fellowship with visiting ministers and other guests in the home.

5

Ethics in Leadership

It's important that a church leader, responsible for the
affairs in God's house, be looked up to—not pushy, not
short-tempered, not a drunk, not a bully, not money-
hungry. He must welcome people, be helpful, wise, fair,
reverent, have a good grip on himself, and have a good
grip on the Message, knowing how to use the truth to
either spur people on in knowledge or stop them in
their tracks if they oppose it.
—Titus 1:7-9 MSG

As we consider the various scriptural passages
relating to ministry, pastoral responsibility, and
church leadership, some consistent themes
emerge. Essentially, they are a collection of guidelines for
the development of good ethics. It is imperative that
leaders live by a well-defined code of ethics. It is
understood that leaders lead! If they will lead, others will
follow.

Followers will emulate the character and characteristics of their leaders. When good ethics are modeled, good conduct results. When leaders are ethical examples, followers will most likely practice ethics.

However, when leaders feel they are above ethical guidelines, "the rules don't apply to me," then the followers are confused by the lack of consistent ethical conduct. When there are no clear examples to follow, leadership is weakened and chaos results.

Paul wrote to Titus similar instructions as to those he had written to Timothy (_1 Timothy 3:1-7, See comments beginning on page 52_). He defined his purpose for leaving Titus in Crete; that he should appoint church leaders and straighten out any remaining problems.

For this reason I left you in Crete, that _you should set in order the things that are lacking,_ and appoint elders in every city as I commanded you; if a man is _blameless, the husband of one wife, having faithful children_ not accused of dissipation or insubordination.

For a bishop must be _blameless,_ as a steward of God, not _self-willed,_ not _quick-tempered,_ not _given to wine,_ not _violent,_ not _greedy for money,_ but _hospitable,_ a _lover of what is good, sober-minded, just, holy, self-controlled, holding fast the faithful word_ as he has been taught, that he may be able, by sound doctrine, both _to exhort and convict_ those who contradict (Titus 1:5-9).

In addition to several of the requirements written to Timothy, Paul adds three other qualities: just, holy, and not self-willed.

Comparison of Paul's Leadership Qualifications

1 Timothy 3:1-7	Titus 1:5-9
blameless	blameless
husband of one wife	husband of one wife
temperate	self-controlled
sober-minded	sober-minded
of good behavior	a lover of what is good
hospitable	hospitable
able to teach	that he may be able, … to exhort
not given to wine	not given to wine
not violent	not violent
not greedy for money	not greedy for money
gentle	
not quarrelsome	not quick-tempered
not covetous	
one who rules his own house well, having his children in submission with all reverence	having faithful children not accused of dissipation or insubordination
not a novice	
a good testimony	
	not self-willed
	just
	holy

To be *self-willed* is to be prideful and could be compared with the warning in 1 Timothy 3:6, "not a novice, lest being puffed up with pride he fall into the *same* condemnation as the devil." Understanding our calling and our position of responsibility as *under-shepherds,* we must resist the temptation to assume authority for the sake of power or prestige. Positions and promotion usually come to those who are past the point of coveting the post just for the *glory*. It doesn't take long to realize that positions require a lot of work and have an abundance of stress associated with the title.

The servant leader must be one who leads from submission and not selfish motivation. Jesus taught that true greatness comes to those who become great servants.

> But he who is *greatest among you shall be your servant*. And whoever exalts himself will be humbled, and he who humbles himself will be exalted (Matthew 23:11-12).

Jesus condemned leadership that exercises authority using position to *lord over* one's subjects. He emphatically stated, "It shall not be so among you." His example provides our model for leadership—we are called to serve.

> But Jesus called them to Himself and said, "You know that the rulers of the Gentiles lord it over them, and those who are great exercise authority over them. Yet *it shall not be so among you;* but whoever desires to become great among you, let him be your servant.
>
> And whoever desires to be first among you, let him be your slave – just as *the Son of Man did not come to be served, but to serve,* and to give His life a ransom for many (Matthew 20:25-28).

Servant Leadership

If you are seeking to serve, ethical principles will come naturally and easily. These principles will help make the choices that foster good character second nature.

Servant leadership is unselfish. It is living for the other person, rather than for yourself. In servant leadership, everything you do is driven by an innate desire to help others, to point them away from you toward Christ. If you do not desire glory for yourself, your motives for serving others will be in the proper perspective. Ethical situations will become easier to detect because *the right thing to do* is the thing to do.

Servant leadership is compassionate and forgiving. It gives others a chance to make mistakes and learn from them. When you hear, "I was set up," it usually has a negative connotation. With servant leadership you love people so much that you set them up for success. When someone drops the ball and makes a mess of a project, who is more qualified to fix it? I guarantee the person who bungled the job is the person who knows first hand what *not* to do. Jesus forgave the sinful woman caught in adultery and sent her on her way to *sin no more*. He gave her a second chance to do the job of moral living right. Some have suggested that this woman was the same

> **Ethical situations will become easier to detect because *the right thing to do* is the thing to do.**

Mary that wept with Jesus at the tomb of her brother, Lazarus. If that was the case, she indeed learned from the Master of forgiveness.

Jesus could have been condescending, being God manifested in human flesh, but that was as contrary to His character as a sinful nature. Is it possible to serve and demean at the same time? Jesus said, "If you do this unto the least of these you have done it unto me" (Matthew 25:40). Treating a subordinate with the same respect we reserve for a superior is rare indeed. If we practice servant leadership we are serving those under us with the same enthusiasm as we serve those over us. This is a true example of servant leadership. There is nothing to gain for ourselves; it is all for the benefit of those we lead.

Jesus Christ was the ultimate example of servant leadership.

Jesus Christ was the ultimate example of servant leadership. He had no thought for himself. Every divine act and mighty miracle He worked solely for others. His mission was foremost on his mind during every event of His life. As a result, He accomplished what He came to do. His every move was orchestrated by principles that were woven into the fabric of His nature. Truth, love, honesty, mercy, compassion, and even judgment were characteristics based on the fact that He was God in flesh. He was tempted, just as we are, and He showed us how to overcome the enemy in that event. He was flesh and experienced every frailty, but He also humbly accepted his destiny. He led us to the cross. He showed us how to live, lead, and die. What a profound example that serves as a pattern for our leadership. Every minister whether man or woman, old or young can experience effective leadership when patterned after Jesus Christ.

Women in Leadership

For a woman, the task of ministering to or pastoring men can be intimidating. God uses women for specific purposes in His kingdom. There were women in the Bible that God ordained for specific purposes.

- Rahab provided refuge for two Israelite spies and thus she and her family were spared during the destruction of Jericho. (See Joshua 2.)

- Deborah was a judge in Israel. God used her as a deliverer during a time of war. (See Judges 4-5.)

- Esther was chosen to be a queen in Persia, and was used in that capacity to spare her people from slaughter. (The Book of Esther.)

- Lydia's hospitality was irresistible to Paul and Silas. After they were released from prison, it was Lydia's home they went to for encouragement before departing from Philippi (Acts 16:13-15, 40).

- Priscilla and Aquilla, a husband and wife team, showed Apollos "the way of God more accurately" (Acts 18:24-26).

- Philip's four daughters prophesied (Acts 21:9).

There are many other biblical accounts of women being used in various ministries. The prophet Joel predicted that "daughters" would prophesy (Joel 2:28-29; Acts 2:17). Peter declared the fulfillment of this prophecy on the day of Pentecost.

Women should not fear the call of God. He always equips those He calls. God will give you the tools to accomplish any job He calls you to do. When He calls someone, man or woman, to His work, He never negates that call. God never goes back on His will concerning the purpose of one's life.

Circumstances may change and doors of opportunity to minister in one area may close, but the call for service never changes. God will provide a new outlet for ministry if we make ourselves available.

A pastor's or missionary's widow may feel disoriented and disconnected with ministry after losing her mate. Her ministry is not finished. It may just be headed in a new direction. While married, her ministry was following the calling of her spouse. Now she must seek to find a place of ministry for her own life.

Some years ago, a missionary became very ill and was forced to come back to the United States to recover. It took many months to recover from the illness and this precious servant was notified that he would never be able to return to the mission field. Yes, it was a very disappointing, dark time, but rather than give in to dismay and just close the door on all opportunity waiting to die, the mission call drove the man to a great work in his native country. Every person he met, every opportunity he had to share this precious truth was met with enthusiasm. Many of the people he won to the Lord never knew how he yearned for the mission field; he fulfilled his mission here.

Women who feel a call to ministry will find an outlet for it. Opportunities are becoming more prevalent as attitudes toward women in ministry are changing. There will always be some men who cannot accept a woman in any ministering capacity. This is not the general consensus, however. In fact, many pastors, bishops, and church leaders are urging women to do more than occupy the church pews and get involved in ministry. Women are being encouraged to give Bible studies and get involved in winning souls. They have been given the authority to work in leadership roles all over the world.

> **Women who feel a call to ministry will find an outlet for it.**

When a woman knows she is called of God to do a service that involves assuming a position of authority, she must obey and submit to God, the Supreme Authority. You may face unexpected challenges associated with your gender, but keep your attitude right, your trust in God, and face each challenge with enthusiasm. God will go with you each step of the way. He is the one who called you—He is the one who opened the door of opportunity for you. A woman in a ministerial position may have God's approval, but in order to gain and keep the male respect, ethical guidelines are a must.

Remember first and foremost that you are a lady. Feminine charm is very becoming to a lady. People are not impressed with a woman who insists on being aggressive, tough, and boisterous. A woman who knows her place and is comfortable in it will experience much more liberty in ministry than one who pushes her way in a masculine manner.

Remember Your Mission

Ask yourself, "What am I here for? What is the bottom line of my calling?" Seek to fulfill your mission in every capacity possible. The pulpit ministry is a very small portion of active ministry. There are godly women who are highly used in the gifts that have never preached a sermon from a podium once in their lives. They are respected among others, effective witnesses, trained teachers, and exuberant evangelists. If you were to ask one, "are you a preacher?" she would probably respond, "no, I'm not a preacher but I am a minister of the gospel." You can be a minister and not a preacher. But you cannot be a preacher without being a minister. If you are a preacher, don't forget the responsibility that comes with the larger portion of your ministry, which is serving others.

A minister with a servant's attitude need not fear stepping out from under the umbrella of authority. She will have no thought for building her own kingdom, but for furthering the Kingdom of God. When a woman leads by serving, she fulfills the leadership philosophy of Jesus Christ. Who better for a mentor and example? When things begin to spin out of control, pressure mounts and you feel you are about to cave in, remember your mission.

You are here to serve. God has called you, and He will strengthen you. His strength is made perfect in our weakness. (See 2 Corinthians 12:9.)

Empowered through Submission

It may be tempting to skip this section. I encourage you to read on especially if you don't want to. Submission has been deeply misunderstood. In the past, the word *submission* has had a negative effect on most women. Men and woman both have a hard time understanding that submission is not an action word, but a philosophy of life. Everyone is submitted to someone. Jesus told the younger person to submit to the elder. In the very next sentence he commanded that everyone be submissive to each other (1 Peter 5:5). Submission is not a gender specific word. It is for all of us. Once anyone understands that submission is as much a part of the Christian life as forgiveness and humility, he or she is prepared to launch into the most extraordinary experience of freedom.

Submission is not a gender specific word. It is for all of us.

Even though a woman usually works under a man, her ultimate authority is God. However, in order to be pleasing to God, a woman must work within the boundaries of God's authority. The principles of submission applied to a woman's life empowers her to work within a window of liberty that otherwise is not possible. If she is single, she answers to her father, pastor, or as a minister, her presbyter, or another to whom she is accountable. If she is married, she must be submissive to her husband, whether he is in the ministry or not.

A godly man, though not called to preach, can empower his wife to fulfill the purpose of God in her life. With that in mind, the woman is given the authority to follow her calling. There is safety in submission to authority. Her husband is a safe place, someone she can go to for advice, counsel, and encouragement.

God will bless you when you cheerfully work under the umbrella of authority. God will also bless your husband with wisdom as you seek his direction. In him you will find reassurance when you are unsure of the next facet of your ministry. Include your husband in your decisions and plans. You may find that he is more interested and willing to be a part of your ministry than you imagined.

There is safety in submission to authority.

The pulpit is a powerful place. We must be careful what we say in the pulpit because of the awe and respect that is rendered anyone who stands behind the podium. Other women can detect an attitude that says, "I answer only to God." Although this may be true in a sense, the attitude is all wrong. An independent attitude may spark feelings of rebellion in others that ignite into fire, destroying God's precious handmaidens. If you have a pulpit ministry, pray that you exude a meek and submissive spirit that empowers other women. Help other women understand that they too can be used of God and still be submissive to their authority.

Be Willing to Pay the P-R-I-C-E

A woman minister may be misunderstood, misrepresented, and sometimes belittled by others when she is simply trying to do the will of God. To compensate for these disadvantages, she must remember there is a price to pay for the road she travels. If she is willing to pay this *price*, she will find contentment in her calling.

> **P—Pressure** - She must be willing to withstand the pressure put on her, not only by men, but by other women that may be jealous of her ministry. There will be scheduling pressures that she must work out. As long as she is prepared and knows that pressure is something that goes with the territory, she will be flexible enough to survive until the pressure lessens a bit or leaves completely.

> **R—Resistance** - She will feel resistance from other ministers. Some men (and women) may never accept her ministry. That is alright. She does not minister to seek the approval of others. Her first obligation is to God and then to the man she is in submission to (either her husband; father, if unmarried; or pastor, if older and unmarried).

> **I—Indifference** - There are times when indifference comes from friends you thought were supportive. It is vital to remember no one sees your vision like you do. Your enthusiasm can only be

imparted by the words you speak and the attitude with which you deliver your burden. It is easy to mistake indifference for rejection when you are the target. If you find friends that were once supportive becoming less enthusiastic about your work, do not grow weary. Find another common ground with those who have lost interest and share your enthusiastic, ministerial ambitions with others dedicated to the same cause as you.

C—Criticism – Donald Rumsfeld, the Secretary of Defense in the Bush Administration said, "If you are _not_ criticized, you may not be doing much."[19] Criticism can be a blessing in disguise. When someone criticizes you, first ask yourself if it is valid. If it is not, and it is basically untrue, then don't worry about it. Just forget it. Untrue statements are not worth losing any sleep over. On the other hand, if there is some substantial proof that the criticism is true and there indeed is room for improvement, accept it graciously and begin to evaluate how you can improve in that area. Criticism can be constructive, if the person receiving it can stay focused on self- improvement.

E—Envy – It may be difficult immediately to identify someone who envies you. Envy is like an ulcer. It eats away at the soul. Eventually, it shows up on the outside. When you encounter someone

---

[19] The Quotations Page, on-line: accessed July 6, 2005; available from http://www.quotationspage.com/subjects/criticism.

who is jealous of you, the best counter action is to be real. Treat people kindly and with respect, even if they have not done so to you. It robs them of further ammunition when you offer them the olive branch of kindness rather than the sword of retribution.

Don't be Intimidated

The Holy Ghost has endowed YOU with limitless potential. As long as you stay true to God, the sky is the limit! Others may try to push you down, making them look better, but God knows your heart. Remember your mission and who called you. If you find yourself constantly being intimidated by a particular person, draw confidence from God and His word. Pour yourself into your calling. Ask God for wisdom to deal with others that have difficulty with your position. You cannot change their minds; let God handle them, and just keep being a gracious lady.

> The Holy Ghost has endowed YOU with limitless potential.

You do not have to feel intimidated if you work among great minds. Thank God for your intellectual mind. It is a great compliment to all women when one with a great mind uses it. It is exciting for someone to compliment you on a well thought-out project, or a tremendous sermon. God blessed you with an intellectual mind in order to put a systematic message together. He helps you keep a focused thought and follow through with an application. Then He anoints the effort and draws the people in the congregation to Him. This is an anointing from God. It is His anointing that puts life into your words and brings success to your efforts. If you begin to rely on your own talents, the purpose is lost. You will find confidence to help you overcome intimidation when you rely upon the Giver of your gifts and not upon your gifts from the Giver.

> Who also _made us sufficient as ministers of the new covenant,_ not of the letter but of the Spirit; for the letter kills, but the Spirit gives life (2 Corinthians 3:6).

Emotional Intelligence

Women have _emotional intelligence_—a wonderful asset when working with people. Being emotional is being sensitive to others needs. When you are accused of being emotional, thank the Lord that you are a woman and that He made you that way. This beautiful trait helps you reach others with your heart, rather than your head. However, just because women are emotional they must not neglect their brains. The employment of intelligence _and_ the passion of emotion is a most effective combination.

Refrain from using emotion to acquire an advantage. There is nothing more irritating than a woman who cries to get her way. Men usually do not know what to do when a woman cries. They cannot relate to the emotional flood, because they don't experience emotion in the same manner. Often, they will do anything to stop the tears. That is the fix-it solution—whatever it takes to stop the crying. But once they catch on to the game, beware. It may have worked in the past, but it may never work again.

Using emotion as a selfish tool degrades the integrity of a woman. Stay in control and talk through situations. Convince someone to your way of thinking by using your intelligence, rather than your tears. It is much more effective. Never use emotion to manipulate. It degrades femininity and robs the person using it of self-control.

The positive side of emotion can be very beautiful. "Plug in" to other's feelings through emotion (co-workers, boss, pastor, pastor's wife, church members, students, etc.). It can be used to your advantage when you reach out to people and empathize with them.

Unlike men, women have to be given authority. According to God's principle of authority, they not come by it naturally. God gives man authority over the woman, and she is given authority from there. The key words here are, "given authority." When you are given something, you must reach out and grasp it. Take the authority you have been given and with feminine uniqueness enhance the job God intended you to do.

6

Etiquette for Service

All Scripture *is* given by inspiration of God,
and *is* profitable for doctrine, for reproof, for correction,
for instruction in righteousness,
that the man of God may be complete,
thoroughly equipped for every good work.
—2 Timothy 3:16-17

Conducting public worship services is an important facet of ministry. Weekly worship is a tradition that predates the Christian church. From Creation there was instituted a day of rest, and from the giving of the Law a Sabbath was observed. Since the initial believers were Jewish with long traditions of weekly observances, it was natural that the new church born on the Day of Pentecost would adopt a similar schedule. Very early in their traditions, they began to meet on the first day of the week. Initially, it was to observe a weekly remembrance of the resurrection of the Lord. As the church developed, a separate day of observance quickly became a distinction between the believers in Christ and Judaism.

While reading and discussion of the words of Scripture was a part of early gatherings, *preaching* has evolved through time into a communicative art form. Preaching styles are much different today than the first century proclamation of the Gospel. Without debating the merits (or detriments) of the changes that have taken place, let us focus on the traditions as we now have them. People have a certain expectation of what a preacher is to do in a worship service, though that typical role varies among different denominations and in various parts of the country.

Carefully crafted words are a powerful catalyst to effect change in the heart of the hearer.

Among Spirit-filled churches the pastor/preacher may be quite involved in leading the service as well as the actual preaching of a sermon. There will be times of exhortation, encouragement, or even correction, as the minister addresses needs in the congregation. This is in keeping with the apostle's admonition, "Preach the word; be instant in season, out of season; reprove, rebuke, exhort with all longsuffering and doctrine" (2 Timothy 4:2 KJV). The NLT translates the last portion of that verse, "Patiently correct, rebuke, and encourage your people with good teaching."

The intent of the man of God is to bring about positive change in the lives of people under his ministry.

112

All pulpit ministries should be thoughtfully and prayerfully administered. Carefully crafted words are a powerful catalyst to effect change in the heart of the hearer. Ministers must prepare to use the Word of God effectively, remembering that it is "living and powerful, and sharper than a two-edged sword" (Hebrews 4:12). Words have the power to save or sever, to hurt or heal, to deliver or to destroy. Never enter the pulpit carelessly or *prayerlessly!*

While much attention is given to the role of the preaching ministry, there is much more to being a preacher than filling the pulpit on Sunday. That is not to minimize this responsibility but to emphasize some of the other aspects of the minister's life. Beyond preaching in worship services, he may be teaching in adult Bible classes, new believer's courses, or mid-week Bible studies. Some pastors also conduct teaching seminars for ministers in training.

A preacher must be able to preach and teach. Paul said, "A bishop then must be ... able to teach" (1 Timothy 3:2). The *Great Commission* assumes we will teach, and disciples will be made in the process. It is not so much a command as it is an axiom or a proverb—*this is what will happen among the believers*. The technique of the commission is to teach!

> Go therefore and *make disciples* [or, Go therefore *making disciples*] of all the nations, baptizing them..., *teaching them* to observe all things that I have commanded you; and lo, I am with you

always, even to the end of the age. Amen (Matthew 28:19-20).

Paul also assumes that a preacher will preach!

For since, in the wisdom of God, the world through wisdom did not know God, _it pleased God through the foolishness of the message preached to save those who believe_ (1 Corinthians 1:21).

To be an effective preacher or teacher, study is required. Inspiration, and "off the cuff" exhortation, will only get you by for a time. Before long you will begin to repeat what you have always said and grow stale in your ministry. Constantly renew your spirit. Feed your mind!

Paul urged Timothy, "Be diligent to present yourself approved to God, a worker who does not need to be ashamed, rightly dividing the word of truth (2 Timothy 2:15). The KJV says, "Study to shew thyself approved unto God." If you don't like to read or study, you must undergo some changes in your personal disciplines. To be an effective minister you must spend time in the Word and learn to read and study.

Keep reading. Keep praying. Keep storing it up. Create a vast reservoir of knowledge and inspiration. The more you store in reserve, the more interesting and relevant your speaking, preaching, and teaching will become. Even good fiction works will exercise the mind and increase your ability to tell a story, creating interesting ways to communicate the message.

Balance novels with inspirational books, historical accounts, and self-improvement books. To improve leadership skills read something motivational from John Maxwell or Andy Stanley, something about church growth from George Barna or Rick Warren, or something to help your personal organization like *Ordering Your Private World* by Gordon MacDonald. Watch for recommended books when you attend conferences or when you receive promotions from your denomination's publishers. Look for favorite authors or subjects online at amazon.com or christianbook.com for discounted books and resources. On amazon.com many books are provided with sample pages from the text and a table of contents that will give you a general overview of the book. There are frequently comments from reviewers on popular books that will give you insight of its applicability to your needs. Search on bookfinder.com for hard-to-find or out-of-print books.

Keep your ministry fresh and relevant. It is okay for evangelists to use sermons again and again, but they must have a fresh anointing and purpose for every service. Preaching and teaching can never be routine and ritual. With each message there must be new taste and a spiritual refreshing. Here are some other recommended categories of reading:

- **Recreational reading** – There is nothing as relaxing as a Louis L'amour western! If lawyer stories are more your type, try books by John

Grisham. Read books by Francine Rivers if you enjoy historical novels. Ask your friends for their recommendations.

- **Editorial and news** – Become aware of current events. What is being debated on talk programs and in editorial columns in the papers and magazines? While you don't want to spend your entire sermon discussing current events, a relevant illustration from something everyone is hearing about may drive home the point of your sermon or lesson.

- **Religious trends** – The magazine *Christianity Today* is a great resource to keep up with current trends within the religious community. Many of their articles are available online at www.christianitytoday.com. Try reading perspectives you don't agree with or listen to *National Public Radio* (NPR) to hear viewpoints that often oppose conservative Christian positions. It will help to articulate your position and defend the biblical perspective. Peter wrote that we should, "always *be* ready to *give* a defense to everyone who asks you a reason for the hope that is in you" (1 Peter 3:15).

- **Bibles, theological tomes, and inspirational works** – In addition to books you are studying for a sermon series, seek out inspirational books on a variety of subjects. Occasionally, try reading a "heavy" book of theology. It will make you think! Pick up *Christian Theology*, by Millard J. Erickson or one of Alister E. McGrath's theological works. For Bible reading, try a new translation to give you a fresh look at some familiar passages of Scripture. The *New Living Translation* (NLT) is a fresh, dynamic equivalent translation of Scripture. Try *The Message*, a paraphrase by Eugene Peterson, for a very modern reading of the biblical text.

- **Homiletics and self-help books** – These resources will improve your preaching and will inspire you to be a better person. Read a homiletics book to learn how to construct a better sermon. A message doesn't have to be badly constructed in order to be anointed! God can anoint a well-built sermon as easily as a collection of rambling thoughts, and it is a whole lot easier for people to understand what you are saying. Other books may inspire you in your prayer life, your personal disciplines, or in controlling your diet and making healthy choices.

In the process of building up yourself, you will find that you are building your library. Books are friends, ready to spend time with us when we have the occasion. A volume that you read long ago and that helped you through a difficult time will be waiting there the next time you need to slip it from the shelf and into your heart.

Pick up material and file it in topical folders for future use. Take notes every chance you get. Write who said it and the date quoted. Keep good notes so that you can document quotations and stories you hear.

When you hear of a good book that someone recommends, write it down so you can add it to your library. Organize your sermons and/or songs, either in notebooks or on the computer.

Even preachers need preaching! Attend conferences and seminars where you can be fed and blessed. There is an abundance of regional preaching conferences where you  can go to hear someone preach that will "stir up the gift of God which is in you." Keep the preacher alive! There is nothing like Spirit-inspired preaching that will ignite your own spirit. With the proliferation of internet sites you will find archived preaching and teaching available at any time. A number of churches and conferences are now webcasting live broadcasts of their services on the internet. So, even if you are not able to attend many conferences in person, you can glean from their ministries.

Ministerial Services

Pastoring is more than preaching, substantially more than perfecting one's performance in the pulpit. The local church pastor may be called upon to pray before a ballgame or community event. He may be interviewed to speak on behalf of Christian viewpoints and values. He is often asked to speak at funerals, weddings, and dedications.

He may be asked to baptize a new believer, give a prayer of dedication for a new house, pray the blessing at a birthday, or be the caller at a cake auction. He becomes a man for all occasions.

Pastoral ministry is in some respects less than you anticipate and in most cases, much more than you bargained for. This is not intended to discourage you from pursuing pastoral ministry but to help prepare you for the pastorate.

A minister who carries himself with dignity avoids raucous behavior, shows himself friendly to guests, and is compassionate to the bereaved will be well-thought of, respected, and appreciated. People are proud of a pastor who does not embarrass them in front of their friends at the important times of their lives: weddings, funerals, baptisms, and other special occasions.

> **A minister who carries himself with dignity will be respected and appreciated.**

Beyond the normal worship service and preaching, there are several special services in which a minister needs to be prepared to officiate and speak. A number of ministerial service books are available, which give you suggested outlines and protocol for these events. Every minister should purchase at least one of these books for reference, preparing for the time when he will be called upon to participate in a special event.[20] Following are general guidelines for some very important occasions: funerals, weddings, baptisms, dedications, communion services, and hospital visitations.

1. Funerals

Death is as sure as life. In time, everyone you know will confront the moment of death. It is the one common event that all will face but few are willing to talk about.

> To everything there is a season, A time for every purpose under heaven: *A time to be born, And a time to die*; A time to plant, And a time to pluck what is planted; ... *A time to weep,* And a time to laugh; *A time to mourn,* And a time to dance; (Ecclesiastes 3:1-2, 4).

Funeral Services

Funerals and memorial services need the minister's personal care and presence. One of the most demanding and important services is the funeral. The minister is in charge of the service, the public ceremony, and order of service. The funeral director will take charge of all the practical details and arrangements for the occasion. There is a necessary cooperation between the

---

[20] Recently, I have recommended *Foster's Ministry Manual*, by Fred Foster, West Monroe, LA, 1996. Another I have used for years is a *Minister's Manual*, by William Piktorn, (Springfield, MO: Gospel Publishing House).

two professionals to have a meaningful service and well-organized ceremony. Cultivate a relationship with local funeral service providers. Get to know the funeral directors on a personal level. When you need their services they will provide a lot of help and support.

In the time of loss, the careful attention of the minister is needed more than at any other event of life. The mere fact of his/her presence will bring immeasurable comfort to the grieving families. It is not that the minister has all the answers or even has much to say; just, "I'm praying for you," or "we love you" can prove to be a tremendous comfort. The following points may serve as a guide to the proper response when learning of a death:

- **Be there as soon as possible** – There is nothing more comforting than having someone you respect come to be with you in your loss. The presence of the minister may serve as a subtle reminder that God is there with you in your darkest hour.

- **Listen with compassion** – "Weep with those who weep." If they are ready to talk, let them. If they are angry and bitter, hear them out. It is important to allow them to vent their emotions in the time of grief. It is impossible to explain death. There are some tragedies that occur in life that we will never be able to understand, but we can share the pain of the moment and continue to trust God in the unknown.

- **Pray and read a Scripture** – There is comfort and strength in our faith. Offer to read a verse of Scripture and pray with them. Selections from the Psalms become favorite passages when one is suffering loss. Psalm 23 is probably the most quoted of all, "Yea, though I walk through the valley of the shadow of death, I will fear no evil; For You *are* with me" (vs. 4).

- **Support their plans** – Encourage them to begin making plans for the memorial or funeral soon after the initial shock is over. A lot of decisions must be made in the first few hours after a death. Don't make the decisions for them, but support them as they choose the way they will remember the departed loved one.

- **Note their plans** – In the case of a sudden and unexpected death there may be no pre-planning for the funeral. Extended illness may allow a person time to plan the funeral service in advance. Others may have pre-arranged the memorial and left detailed instructions behind for their service. Once a funeral home is chosen, the director will assist in setting the time and place of the service. A time for visitation (wake or viewing) must be decided, musical selections or Scripture readings must be selected, and the minister and/or others appointed to speak must be notified. Decisions for the grave service and location for interment will have to be made.

- **Verify facts for the obituary** – A brief outline of important information will be needed for the newspaper and funeral program obituary, including birth date and place, places of residence, important achievements, church membership, survivors (family members), and the time of death. Some families like to compile a memorial program with a more detailed history, while others include some favorite photographs or poetry. The family may wish to prepare a video or computer presentation of memories for the service.

- **Be present at the visitation** – It is suggested that the minister arrive at the funeral home early, before the family visitation. Meet the family for prayer and be with them the first time they see the casket and gather for the viewing.

- **Be aware of cultural customs** – Local customs vary from one region of the country to another, from one ethic group to another. Will they plan a wake? Will they have a visitation? Open casket or closed? Many traditions have a dinner for family and friends after the graveside service.

The funeral service is a formal occasion. It is always appropriate for the minister to wear a suit. While a black suit has long been the funeral tradition, any darker colored suit with conservative shirt and tie will be acceptable.

Make sure shoes are polished and shirt and suit are clean and pressed. Look your best!

The officiating minister should never be late for a funeral service. Plan on being there a half-hour before you expect the family to arrive. That way, if you are a little late and they are a little early, you will be there to meet them.

Meet with the family before the funeral service. Take time to explain the procedure for the day. Information can be comforting. If they know what to expect in the service, there is a feeling of order and structure in a time of emotional chaos. Have prayer with the family before entering the auditorium, if it is a church funeral. In a funeral home you may be able to meet them in the family room, usually located to one side of the chapel.

Give comfort and hope in the promises of Scripture.

Made sure each participant is given an "order of service." Musicians, singers, other ministers, and the funeral director need to know what order will be followed and where they come in. It is not necessary to emcee the funeral and introduce each participant, if each one knows when to speak, sing, or play. When the family desires to allow a time for friends to come forward to speak on the behalf of the deceased, suggest a time limit for this open forum. A gentle reminder in the service to keep remarks brief may help avoid a marathon memorial service.

Be considerate of the time during the service. The funeral is not an occasion to give an extended homily demonstrating your knowledge of Scripture. Make your remarks relevant and personal. You do not have to save or condemn the departed; just preach the hope of the Gospel to the living. Give comfort and hope in the promises of Scripture. When people are touched with grief they are more vulnerable to the Spirit of God and receptive to life-changing decisions. They need to hear the truth of the Gospel that will prepare all to face death.

At the conclusion of the service and after the closing prayer, stand at the head of the casket for the final viewing by the congregation. (Some may choose to have the viewing only before the service.) Hold your Bible in your right hand to discourage handshaking. Sometimes it becomes sort of a greeting line. Don't refuse to shake hands if someone reaches out to you, just discourage it as much as possible.

After the congregation has filed passed the deceased and they are out of the building, the family has their last moments with the body before the casket is closed and taken to the cemetery. This is an intimate time with the family members. The minister should stand with them for comfort and support.

When the funeral director indicates that it is time to leave, the minister should lead the procession (after the funeral director clears the way) to the hearse and remain there until the hearse is closed. He should follow (or meet) the hearse at the cemetery and be prepared to lead the way to the gravesite. He will take his position at the head of the coffin and make final remarks and a Scripture reading.

Another prayer is appropriate before concluding this brief service. The minister will then lead the way for friends to greet the family and offer condolences.

A more exhaustive planning guide for weddings and funerals can be found in _The Pastor's Guide to Weddings & Funerals_, by Victor D. Lehman.[21] The _Federal Trade Commission_ provides a good resource for the legal regulations governing funeral homes and gives helpful planning information entitled "Funerals: A Consumer Guide" on their website. Go to www.ftc.gov and search for the document or carefully enter the web address given in the footnote.[22]

2. Weddings

Some ministers say that weddings are the most challenging services they conduct. It is indeed a stressful time for the bride and groom, as well as others involved in the planning of the service and the occasion itself. There

are a variety of expectations for the family members present, and some are not shy about voicing their opinions as to how this service should be conducted. Of course, every one wants the occasion to be perfect and the couple to be hitched, _without a hitch!_

---

[21] Victor D. Lehman, _The Pastor's Guide to Weddings & Funerals_, (Valley Forge, PA: Judson Press, 2001).

[22] http://www.ftc.gov/bcp/conline/pubs/services/funeral.htm

Meet the couple who wants to be married to discuss church policy, pre-marriage counseling sessions, and to establish a date for the ceremony. Church policy may be developed to cover issues like cleaning deposits, dress regulations, use of candles, sound equipment and any charges associated with the use of the facility. Having a *church use policy* is especially important if your facility is one that couples from the community desire to rent for their weddings. If the couple are members of your church, you may choose to reduce the rental fee or to waive all charges.

The pastor or a designated minister should set up pre-marriage counseling for the couple. The number of sessions will depend on you. You may only want to meet them once or twice and recommend other resources to read. You may want to guide them through the subjects you feel are most important to a long-lasting marriage. Subjects that should be addressed are compatibility, family backgrounds, finances, budgeting, family planning, and expectations in the marriage. Some of the resources at the conclusion of this book (Page 245) can serve as a guide or assist you in developing these sessions.

It should not be the minister's place to give advice on sex. He should not be viewed as the *sex expert*. He may give more general instruction on the beauty of sexuality from a biblical viewpoint and emphasize its sacredness in marriage. I have often recommended *The Act of Marriage and the Beauty of Sexual Love* by Tim and Beverly LaHaye for a couple to read just before marriage.

Some couples may want to write their own vows. This is fine as long as you are comfortable with the final draft and they maintain the appropriate commitment based on biblical values. If you are apprehensive about it, schedule a time when you can assist them in writing their vows. That way you can make suggestions, feeling a little more in control of the outcome and yet allowing them to compose their own vows.

The focus of the marriage ceremony should be on the bride and groom. It is important to maintain that they are the most important part of the service. Their wishes and desires should be the first considered. If you see that a bride is being pressured or forced to do something against her will, it may be that you are the only one who can intervene. As a minister, you usually are afforded a higher level of respect, even from those who are not of the same faith. This is not to be taken lightly or abused, but it can be a source of convenient leverage when dealing with an overly manipulative relative.

> As a minister, you usually are afforded a higher level of respect, even from those who are not of the same faith.

You may have someone in the church that is good with organizational skills that you could assign as a _wedding coordinator_. This is someone who can meet with and explain church policy to those who wish to have wedding ceremonies conducted in your facility. When looking for someone to be a wedding coordinator, you will need to find one who is not afraid to take charge; someone with the initiative to follow through. She helps the bride coordinate her plans with your schedule. She can clear up many questions regarding church wedding guidelines, give the bride and groom suggestions on music, the reception, and decorations. The wedding coordinator is invaluable to help plan the wedding, walking the couple step by step through the rehearsal and ceremony.

The coordinator will work closely with you during the rehearsal. She is available to see that it starts on time and goes smoothly. Although you are responsible for the ceremony etiquette and will be the primary spokesman, it is nice to have a liaison between the bride and well-meaning family members or friends if things start to get out of hand. Providing the services of someone else with knowledge about weddings can help preserve the couple's wishes. Then if the couple needs you to intervene, you can do so with the support of your church coordinator.

When it is time for the ceremony, the coordinator will help pin corsages, keep mom calm, tell bridesmaids when to enter the procession and help the bride with last minute touches before entering the sanctuary.

Since the minister is essentially responsible for the ceremony, he should be ready to take charge if something goes wrong—for example, if an attendant faints, if someone gets sick, or if children become out of control. In one wedding we attended, the bride almost fainted during the ceremony. She gracefully sank to her knees just as the minister asked for the vows to be repeated. The minister did a tremendous job keeping things in order. When the bride regained her composure, he addressed the audience with a tasteful amount of humor that put everyone at ease.[23]

It is usually the groom's task to secure the marriage license, though both parties must apply in person. The legal requirements for marriage vary from state to state. Check with the local county (or parish) clerk's office for the requirements in your area. It would be good to have a copy of the regulations to give to prospective grooms. Many areas of the country now post the requirements and procedures for obtaining a marriage license online, usually on the county government website. This will include information like:

- Whether or not blood tests are required.

- If the bride and groom must be residents in the state.

- If there is a waiting period between the time when a marriage license is obtained and the ceremony.

- How long the license is valid before the ceremony.

---

[23] For a complete wedding guide, see *To Have and To Hold, Wedding Planner*, by Gayla M. Baughman, (Pleasanton, CA: Baughman Group Ministries, 2002).

- Regulations on the format of the marriage ceremony.

- Who may marry (age, divorced, sexes, etc.).

- If witnesses are required.

- If *common law* or marriage by *proxy* is allowable in the state.

- The cost of the license.

- If the minister must be registered in the state.

3. Baptisms

Family members who are not normally in attendance at your church will frequently come for a special occasion to which they have been invited. The *baptism* of a family member is one such occasion that may produce a number of visitors. Scheduled baptismal services can thus be used to the advantage of introducing new people to the church. The setting provides an  opportunity to explain the beauty of water baptism and the story of salvation to those assembled. Appropriate remarks to the candidate for baptism should be prepared and a brief explanation of why we baptize in Jesus' name would be helpful.

Make *water baptisms* special, sacred times. Know that you are cooperating with God to see their sins washed away!

The following are some general guidelines for baptismal services:

- Make sure the tank is filled with clean water and the water temperature is comfortable.

- Either provide baptismal robes for the candidates or have them bring a change of clothes and towels.

- Explain what you are going to do and then pray with the candidate.

- Have the candidate hold his nose and mouth with one hand and his wrist with the other. Place one hand on the back of the candidate and the other over his hand at the wrist.

- Recite a baptismal statement, something like, "Upon the confession of your faith, I now baptize you in the name of the Lord Jesus Christ for the remission of sins." While the exact wording of a baptismal statement is not given in Scripture, it is essential to recite "in the name of Jesus" in your declaration. Nowhere in Scripture was anyone in the church baptized in any other name (Acts 4:12).[24]

---

[24] See other instances of baptism in the New Testament church: Acts 2:38-41; Acts 8:12-16; Acts 10:47-48; Acts 19:1-6; Acts 22:16; Romans 6:1-4; Galatians 3:27; Colossians 3:17. All of these were

- Gently ease the candidate back into the water completely submerging him or her. The natural force of the water will begin to push back. Let this natural fluid movement help you; as the water returns raise the candidate back up. Some newer baptismal tanks have a built-in seat. This makes it easier to baptize without creating a tidal wave!

- Encourage the candidate to worship and thank the Lord for sins remitted.

4. Dedications

Dedications of Children are a very important time to the new parents. Make them special. You can tailor the service to the family (or families) participating. *Child dedications* will bring out the extended family, dressed in their finest, when the pastor provides a special day and appropriate message for the newborn. Parents are vulnerable to their God-given responsibility in the time when they are marveling at the miracle of a new birth and may be positively encouraged in the development of  their relationship with God. Some child dedications may

written with an understanding of the intent of the commission of Matthew 28:19.

be designed for older children of new believers in the congregation who desire to present their children to the Lord.

If the entire service is given to the dedication of a child (or children), a sermon may be selected that emphasizes the blessing of children or the importance of parenting. When it is time for the dedication portion of the service, have the family (or families) bring their child (or children) to the front. You may want to comment on the child and family. Offer a brief biblical application and lead in prayer. Some hold the infant for prayer and then return him/her to the parents. This is symbolic of giving the child to the Lord and then receiving him, as loaned from God to raise and nurture in the Lord. Appropriate songs are "Jesus Loves the Little Children," "Yes, Jesus Loves Me," or similar selections.

While a *church dedication* service is designed more for the membership, it may afford an opportunity to ask city officials and members of your financial institution to  attend. It is also an opportunity to "show off" your new facility to any of the local public and members from other churches who may be interested. Some churches choose to have a *grand-opening* for the public where they invite city officials and business people who have helped make the dream come true, and have a separate *dedication* service for the church family to devote their new facility to the work of the Lord. A church dedication is an opportunity to remind the membership of the significance of reverencing the building as the "house of God" and emphasizing the importance of God's blessing and favor on everything that is housed in the facility.

While singing, worship, and preaching may be included in this service, it tends to be a little more formal when you have invited guests and have designated time for special recognitions and acknowledgements. This is an important time to recognize the contribution and labor of all involved.

The choir or special singing group may prepare selections reflecting the dedication. The pastor or special speaker may have the congregation pray for various parts of building—laying hands on the furnishings and walls to participate in a prayer of dedication. Some use a recitation where the congregation responds with a pledge to dedicate the house of the Lord. See an example in *Foster's Ministry Manual*, page 101. For information on this and other resources, see page 245.

5. Communion

The *Communion* service is a sacred time of remembrance for what Christ has done to bring salvation. A well-prepared message and well-planned service can be *remembered*, as well as being an appropriate *remembrance*.

Developing after the pattern of the ancient Jewish Passover, the observance of the *Lord's Supper* or *Communion* holds a rich tradition in Scripture. The Hebrew Passover commemorated the deliverance of the nation from Egyptian slavery. It also anticipated the future blessing in the Messianic Age. Paul incorporated the images of the Jewish Passover in the Christian communion in 1 Corinthians 5:6-8. He declared that "Christ, our Passover, was sacrificed for us."

It was in a Passover observance, the Last Supper, that Jesus gave the pattern for the memorial. When supper was completed He presented the symbols of the bread and wine to represent His body and blood. Jesus said the bread is, "My body, which is given for you" and the fruit of the vine is the "new covenant in my blood, which is shed for you" (Luke 22:20).

There are two dimensions of the communion service. One dimension is as a memorial: "Do this in remembrance of me" (Luke 22:19). The other dimension is eschatological, anticipating the return of the Lord, "till he comes" (1 Corinthians 11:26).

The communion service reflects on His sacrifice and celebrates His life, remembers the cost of the cross and anticipates the hope of salvation. Each communion service links the historical event with the future hope. Communion should not be seen as a morbid replay of Christ's tragic death, but a reflection of hope in His eternal purpose.

There is no specified schedule for the observance of communion. Paul said, "For as often as you eat this bread and drink this cup." Some churches have an annual observance (often in a watch-night service), while others have quarterly, monthly, or even weekly communion services. Too frequent services, however, may reduce the sacredness of the occasion and cause it to be more of a routine ritual.

The following guidelines may assist you in coordinating a communion service that will be both spiritual and inspirational:

- Do not rush the ceremony. Allow a solemn and sacred atmosphere of reflection and consecration to develop.

- Use a spiritual leader in the church to assist in this service.

- Organize the service in advance so everything is ready and all involved know what is expected of them.

- Use appropriate music and incorporate a worshipful atmosphere in the service.

- Explain that the service is "open communion" but intended for believers. Some denominations do not allow non-members to participate.

- Read from the Gospels concerning the Last Supper or Paul's instructions in Corinthians. (See Matthew 26:17-20, 26-29; Mark 14:12-17, 22-25; Luke 22:7-20; 1 Corinthians 11:23-31)

- Distribute the bread and wine with the help of ushers, or have the people serve themselves as they file by the table.

- Instruct them to hold the bread and cup until the appropriate moment when you will partake together.

- Pray for the bread. Read 1 Corinthians 11:23-24. Eat the bread together.

- Pray for the cup. Read 1 Corinthians 11:25-26. Drink the cup together.

- Allow time for testimony and reflection.

- Conclude with a song of consecration or celebration.

- Dismiss to foot-washing service, if one is planned.

6. Hospital Visitation

Hospitals are not high on the list of entertainment hot spots. People don't go to the hospital for a vacation or for a fun weekend. Their visits are either *preventive*, a  procedure to promote health and avoid disease, or *responsive*, seeking treatment in order to regain health.

For most people the hospital experience is likely to be an emotional upheaval. People are there because of sickness, disease, pain, injury, or trauma. The birth of a child is the happiest reason to be in the hospital, but even in child-bearing, there is the element of danger and promise of pain. This experience is also emotional, with joy in the miracle of new birth and pain in labor—even surgery should there be any complications.

Often when people are affected with illness or facing surgery they are *more responsive* to a pastoral visit and *more open* to discussion of the truly important matters of eternity and salvation. It is during this time that many will listen to the *man of God.* Therefore, visiting the sick must be an urgent task of the ministry. It may be at the door of eternity that the minister will be the one to escort the dying into the kingdom of God rather than eternal damnation.

A minister's compassion in the time of sickness or bereavement will long be remembered by family members in his congregation or community. Lasting bonds of affection are formed during the trauma of tragedy. Walk through the valley with someone and they will never forget your kindness. It is such relationships that build lasting pastorates and make a minister more effective in the church.

Depending on the size of your church and staff the amount of time spent in hospital visitation will vary. In many churches you may go weeks without a call to the hospital and then find yourself making daily trips to see the convalescing. In larger churches there are few times in the year when you or a staff member will not be required to visit the hospital on a weekly (if not daily) basis.

Some pastors enjoy hospital visitation so much they spend many of their days occupied in this area of ministry. Some join the chaplaincy at a local hospital. While this is an important ministry, there needs to be a balance with other ministerial duties and a careful distribution of time.

Hospital Visitation Tips

- Most hospitals rely on volunteers to assist in the information booth. They are not knowledgeable of the condition of the patients or privy to any personal information. They can help you find the right room number and offer directions to the appropriate floor or wing of the medical facility.

- If you know the room number, proceed to the appropriate area of the hospital and stop by the nurses' station to confirm if the patient is in the room and available for a visit.

- Follow directions. You will not gain friends at the hospital by intruding into areas that are off-limits or by ignoring posted regulations. For your own safety it is vital to observe signs. Some patients have communicable diseases or lowered resistance to disease and posted regulations will require you to don mask, rubber gloves, and a sterile gown (over your clothes) to either protect you or the patient. These are usually provided outside the door of the patient's room.

- Do not sit on the hospital bed or jar it. Patients may be in pain. Be aware of the various tubes and instruments monitoring the patient when you touch them or pray with them.

- Keep the visit brief unless the patient asks you to stay longer. Usually the sick need to rest and are frequently interrupted by their care providers. After a casual visit, offer to pray. When appropriate, read a passage of Scripture that will inspire faith or give comfort and assurance.

- Don't ask, don't tell. Use care not to inquire too much about their specific condition. It may be a personal condition that he or she would not be comfortable sharing with you. If the family has revealed that the condition is terminal, find out how much the patient has been told. The severity of the patient's condition should not come from you, unless you have been asked to break the news.

- When possible, observe the posted visiting hours. Clergy privilege may allow you to visit at other times but reserve most of these *privileged visits* to emergencies not as a matter of personal convenience.

- Clergy privileges may include free parking. Some ministerial organizations provide window stickers to identify you as a member of the clergy. You may also offer your business card or ministerial identification to gain access to these privileges.

- Some hospitals may require you to register with the chaplain and obtain an ID badge for use in the hospital, especially if you wish to visit others besides your own church members. You may wish to become a volunteer hospital chaplain. This can be an opportunity to serve in the area of hospital visitation and ministry.

Remember the Shut-ins

Not all patients are in the hospital. There are also _shut-ins_—those who, for medical conditions or physical limitations, are unable to attend church. These should not be shunned nor forgotten in the course of pastoral ministry. Maintain a rotating list of these individuals and make it a point to visit them on a consistent basis. You may also have ministries in the church to provide them with the weekly bulletin, recordings of services, and special mementos of events, so they will continue to feel connected with the congregation and ministered to in their time of need.

Take heed to the ministry which you have received in the Lord, that you may fulfill it (Colossians 4:17).

7

Morality in the Ministry

It is God's will that you should be sanctified: that you should avoid sexual immorality; that each of you should learn to control his own body in a way that is holy and honorable, not in passionate lust like the heathen, who do not know God; and that in this matter no one should wrong his brother or take advantage of him. The Lord will punish men for all such sins, as we have already told you and warned you. For God did not call us to be impure, but to live a holy life.
—1 Thessalonians 4:3-7 NIV

In an increasingly immoral culture, the necessity of maintaining exceptional moral conduct in the ministry is of paramount importance. Even though western society has adopted extremely tolerant and permissive attitudes toward sexuality, the majority still expect Christians, and especially ministers, to maintain exemplary moral conduct and Christian virtues. It is not uncommon for one to say, "I thought she was a Christian" upon hearing rumors of infidelity. The same people who are tolerant and accepting of immoral behavior in themselves or among their friends are quick to condemn such behavior by Christians.

Regardless of cultural acceptance or condemnation of immoral behavior, the Christian is held to a higher standard of morality on the basis of Scripture. Moral principles are biblical and unalterable regardless of the societal shifting of values and widespread acceptance of immoral practices.

Of all subjects taught under the scope of *ministerial ethics,* morality in the ministry is the most vital to your success. Moral failure accounts for many of those who leave the ministry. Immorality is one of the greatest areas of temptation and most frequent faults in the failure of ministers. Men of great influence have fallen overnight with the revelation of improper sexual relationships.

Observe the tide of public sentiment when a well-known televangelist admits to adultery. Ministers are expected to maintain a higher standard of morality than the general church membership. What may be tolerated, or at least forgiven, in others is steadfastly required of the one who is called of God. The following examples are given to illustrate what can happen when a minister yields to immoral temptation:

- A respected minister who had served on the organization's district board for many years had carried on a secret affair with a woman in the church for over a decade. Some of their clandestine meetings had even been in the church. As a member of the board, he sat in judgment of other ministers for adultery while he himself was guilty of the same.

- A growing church and effective pastoral ministry was destroyed when it was discovered that the pastor had secretly visited gay bars in the city. He was caught in a club dancing with other men and was exposed for his double life.

- Another pastor went on frequent *"missionary"* trips to Mexico. He came back with glowing reports of revival and miracles. When he returned from one trip bearing the injuries of a beating, he told stories of persecution and opposition to his *ministry*. The church responded with a greater resolve to continue their support for his work in missions. Eventually, it was discovered that his *missions trips* were actually visits to Las Vegas or Reno, and his beating resulted from being caught with someone else's wife!

The stories are endless, and the tragedies will be repeated. All of these instances are true. Each happened when I was a younger minister and the tragedies strengthened my determination not to be a casualty of this type. Sadly, these are only three occasions out of numerous stories of moral failures I know personally.

I sat across the table at a fast food restaurant while a minister confessed his moral failure to me. I witnessed the failure of his ministry and the destruction of their marriage. His life was shipwrecked by a fling of passion. On other occasions, I have seen the tears of regret on the faces of young people who had to leave their ministerial training program because of moral failure.

I would like to make sure this does not happen to you! My prayer is that you will resolve now, *not* to be a statistic in the fatalities of moral failure. You cannot afford to let

 down your guard for one minute. The enemy of your soul will set a trap for you and ensnare you at the first opportunity, at the slightest demonstration of vulnerability.

Consistent personal ethical conduct and a healthy relationship with your spouse will be the best safeguards for moral purity. Strict guidelines for conduct with members of the opposite sex must become a part of your commitment to purity. I have taught from the following guidelines for so long that I don't remember if I developed them or if they were adapted from another source. Nevertheless, the principles are perennially valid.

Guidelines for Maintaining Moral Purity

1. **Never, Never, Never be alone with a member of the opposite sex.**

    Other than with your spouse or your immediate family, refuse to allow yourself to be caught in a position where you are alone with someone of the opposite sex. Paul exhorted Timothy to "Flee youthful lusts; but pursue righteousness" (2 Timothy 2:22). Any occasion that provokes lustful thoughts and feelings should be a red flag of warning. _Flee_—run away from—any situation that becomes compromising.

Joseph is a sterling example of consistent integrity. Sold into slavery by his brothers at a young age, he was transported many miles from home and eventually became a trusted servant in an Egyptian household. Though he was a great distance from anyone who knew him, he recognized that God was still a witness to his actions. Through every adversity that life brought to him, he maintained respect for God and the awareness that he was accountable ultimately to Him. When his master's wife attempted to seduce him and openly invited him to have sex with her, he refused saying, "How can I do this great wickedness and _sin against God?_" (Genesis 39:9).

The temptation and the attempt to trap Joseph in an immoral act did not stop there. The biblical account continues, revealing that she persisted "day after day" to get him to "lie with her _or_ to be with her" (vs.10). She continued to seduce Joseph and found an occasion when "none of the men of the house was inside" (vs. 11). She sought a time when they could be _alone!_

Potiphar, Joseph's master, left him at home with his wife because he trusted Joseph. There alone, when Joseph rejected her advances, she turned like a venomous snake and accused him of the very act that she herself had propositioned! She screamed "Rape!" as Joseph ran from her clutches leaving his outer robe behind. _Hell has no fury_ *like a woman scorned!*[25] The lust had now turned to hatred, and she plotted to destroy Joseph. When Potiphar returned and heard her tearful tale, he placed Joseph in prison for the alleged offense.

When you are alone with someone, there are no witnesses to defend your good character; it is only your word against hers. Like Joseph, you may suffer the consequences of an action that never took place! Protect yourself. Make it a rule to *never* be alone with a member of the opposite sex.

> ## Make it a rule to *never* be alone with a member of the opposite sex.

Pastors should not go to lunch alone with their secretaries. Refuse to ride in a car alone with a staff member of the opposite sex. If the two of you are going to a meeting, take two cars or get others to accompany you (preferably include your spouse).

I remember hearing an elder minister, David Gray, speak at a chapel service in Bible College. He warned us that even if you see one of your female church members carrying groceries in the rain, do not pick her up if you are alone! He suggested getting someone to come with you or sending someone else to help her. Even if there is no evil intention on either part, you never know the *wagging*

---

[25] From the quotation: "Heaven hath no rage like love to hatred turned, Nor Hell a fury, like a woman scorned" by William Congreve (1670-1729).

tongues who will see you together. "Do not let your good to be spoken of as evil" (Romans 14:16).

2. Never counsel without safeguards.

For the married pastor, one of the best safeguards is to have your spouse present whenever you counsel someone of the opposite sex. For many in ministry, the husband and wife are such a team that it is natural and helpful to have both involved in counseling that may get into areas of intimacy or subjects of a sexual nature.

For the occasion when something comes up in a casual visit or someone asks for your counsel on the spot without setting an appointment for a *counseling session,* other safeguards are helpful. If you are in the office when someone comes by, leave the door open. Do not allow anyone to close the door. If she insists on privacy, set an appointment or bring someone else into the office. You must protect yourself before you protect her secret sin.

Some offices are designed with large windows so that others can see in without being able to hear the conversation. This is helpful for a visual safeguard, but the individual may still be freer to speak things that are inappropriate if she feels that no one else is hearing them. Some, in a private setting, have confessed their infatuation for the pastor or disclosed intimate details of a relationship that did not need to be revealed. Are all the intimate details really necessary to know in your counseling session?

In a pastoral visit, if a woman is sharing her difficulties at home and the lack of attention she is getting from her husband, the pastor's *concern for her* may be misinterpreted as *interest in her.* What may begin innocently as a caring pastor/hurting member relationship may end up being a personal ministry project in a darkened room. *Don't even start down that hall!* Keep your safeguards in place.

3. **Report any proposition or impropriety to your spouse immediately.**

Whenever someone makes an inappropriate suggestion to you, even in a flirtatious way, immediately contact your spouse. Don't wait until later or think that it is not "that big of a deal." Do not allow time to reconsider. The longer you wait to discuss it with your spouse, the more time you have to entertain the suggestion.

If someone makes a pass at you or you are openly propositioned, it is vital to call your spouse, even in the presence of the one who has made the proposition. Show the offending person how committed you are to your marriage vows. When she sees your faithfulness to fidelity she will look elsewhere for cheap thrills or a husband to steal. This type of response to an improper proposal will also help your spouse to see how seriously you take your commitment to her. It works both ways: husband or wife.

One day, Gayla and I were in a large electronics superstore. I was looking at computers while my wife was in another part of the store. She sought me out looking rather upset. A complete stranger had engaged her in conversation and remarked on how good she looked. While I agree with the truth of his comments, she understood that his motivation was impure and she quickly got away from him and came directly to me to share the experience. There is safety in sharing inappropriate remarks and refusing to keep them secret from your spouse.

4. **Constantly cultivate your relationship with your spouse.**

One relatively easy way to maintain your marriage relationship is to plan activities together. A weekly date-night can give you something to look forward to as a special time alone. Even if you are on a limited budget, take an evening to eat fast food or take *peanut butter and jelly* sandwiches to the park! Take a drive or go for a walk through the mall.

> **Plan to go places together; even if it is for business you can make it a getaway.**

Avoid frequent appointments away from home that require you to be separated. Plan to go places together; even if it is for business, you can make it a getaway. I have gone with my wife to ladies' meetings just to be with her. While she was in meetings I worked on another book!

Communicate freely. Share your life and feelings with one another. This may be easier for one spouse, but encourage the other to share thoughts, and then take time to listen. Talk about your fears and frustrations. Share your hopes and dreams. Seek advice from your mate for conflicts on the job or decisions that must be made. Wisdom will come out of these times of collective communication and a side effect will be a closer relationship with your spouse.

5. Keep "touch" purely professional.

Physical touch is a powerful communicator of feelings. To avoid sending the wrong message, the minister should be very aware of *how* and *whom* he touches. In our circles of fellowship the handshake is almost a universal greeting. Women who are acquainted may share a brief hug. As a show of affection men may be comfortable with a pat on the shoulder or an arm around the neck. Some church groups are freer with hugs between men and women. It is a trend I resist because of the familiarity it breeds between men and women.

Contact with the opposite sex should be especially limited.

Any form of contact may be misunderstood at times. Even a lingering handshake can convey emotion! No wonder Paul said, "It is good for a man not to touch a woman" (1 Corinthians 7:1).

Contact with the opposite sex should be especially limited. When anointing someone for prayer, use the finger tips on the forehead. If a man is praying for a woman in the altar he should only touch the woman on the head, or the wrist, if she has raised her hands in prayer. As a general rule there should be *no* touching beyond the head, shoulders, or hands!

In times of grief it may be appropriate to give a pat on the arm or a brief hug around the shoulders, as you offer your condolences. It is less likely that a woman will interpret the minister's touch as being inappropriate when showing compassion in the time of grief.

In every church there are the *huggers* who are completely uninhibited and will grab you in a hug every chance they get. With some people you may want to keep a church pew between you! However, if new converts are so full of the love of the Lord that they spontaneously hug you in the altar, don't embarrass them by rebuking them for their action. Just smile (and blush) and move on! They will adapt to our protocol if they stay around long enough!

Use extra caution around children. Some children are very affectionate and will run to greet you as their pastor. We want to cultivate good and positive relationships with the children of our congregations. However, due in part to the scandals plaguing the Catholic Church, care must be observed that all contact with children be appropriate. If your hug or embrace is misinterpreted, you could face allegations of abuse, molestation, and even a criminal lawsuit. It does not have to be *true* for the media to report it and someone to believe it. Again, the rule is *no* touching beyond the head, shoulders, or hands!

6. Always speak well of your spouse in public.

There should be no doubt in your congregation that you are in love with your spouse. Support her openly and publicly. Express your appreciation and love for her. Refrain from cutting, critical remarks. Criticizing your spouse publicly tells others that you are dissatisfied with your choice.

This may also require you to come to your spouse's defense when someone else is being critical. If you appear to be in agreement with the criticism, that may be interpreted the same as if you were the critical one.

In a marriage relationship you are *one flesh!* If someone is critical of my spouse, they are talking about me. If I am defensive about what they say about me, I should respond in the same way if they are critical of my spouse.

> So then, they are no longer two but *one flesh.* Therefore *what God has joined together, let not man separate* (Matthew 19:6).

7. Moral purity before marriage will go a long way to maintaining purity and trust in the marriage.

If you were sexually involved with your spouse before marriage, she may wonder if you are being faithful to her at some point in the future. Once infidelity takes place there is always a nagging suspicion that it could happen again. That is one reason why trust is so hard to rebuild after an adulterous affair. Obviously, if you find yourself in this position it is impossible to undo the mistakes of the past. You must work to regain trust and submit to accountability with your partner in order to keep the boundaries secure and to reaffirm the commitment to purity.

For young people who are just beginning the journey to a lifetime of ministry, you have a wonderful opportunity to pledge faithfulness to that marriage partner that you have yet to meet. The greatest gift you can give your future spouse is the gift of virtue. A commitment to moral purity will have a lasting reward in the sacredness of your vows to one another on your wedding day.

> **The greatest gift you can give your future spouse is the gift of virtue.**

8. Be sexually committed to your spouse.

Do your homework! If you work to have a good loving relationship with your spouse and keep the passion and excitement in your physical relationship, there is little chance someone else can entice you or your spouse into a sexual tryst. *When you are eating great meals from your own kitchen, you are not tempted with leftovers in the neighbor's trash can!*

Some ministers who have fallen into adultery have admitted to finding in someone else what they were not receiving at home. While this does not excuse immoral conduct, it does underscore the importance of Paul's teaching in his letter to the Corinthians.

Let the husband render to his wife the affection due her, and likewise also the wife to her husband. The wife does not have authority over her own body, but the husband does. And likewise the husband does not have authority over his own body, but the wife does.

Do not deprive one another except with consent for a time, that you may give yourselves to fasting and prayer; and come together again so that Satan does not tempt you because of your lack of self-control (1 Corinthians 7:3-5).

Thank God for the Church at Corinth! While it may be uncomfortable to read about some of the conditions among the Corinthians, we now have some guiding principles to apply to our generation that has embraced every immoral act and perverse practice imaginable. Because of Paul's writing on these subjects, we have some rather straight-forward instructions concerning sexuality and proper conduct in the church.

> **The church was born into adversity and thrived in a hostile culture.**

The New Testament church was not born into Victorian England propriety or into a conscientious Christian culture. The church was born into adversity and thrived in a hostile culture, even without a New Testament! We are equipped and enabled by the Holy Spirit *and* the Word of

God to face any challenge and teach godly principles in a perverse generation.

When one is converted to Christianity, he can no longer follow his own desires. The child of God becomes one with the Lord and must dedicate his spirit and body to the service of the Lord. Our purpose is to glorify God in our *body* and in our *spirit*. It all belongs to God!

> But he who is joined to the Lord is one spirit with Him. *Flee sexual immorality.* Every sin that a man does is outside the body, but he who commits sexual immorality sins against his own body.
>
> Or do you not know that *your body is the temple of the Holy Spirit who is in you,* whom you have from God, and you are not your own? For you were bought at a price; therefore *glorify God in your body and in your spirit,* which are God's (1 Corinthians 6:17-20).

Restoration

After dealing with such an important subject and prevalent problem as sexual immorality, it is appropriate to conclude with a call for restoration. Moral failure is not the *unpardonable sin.* God will forgive the fornicator, the adulterer, and the perverse person. Repentance and surrender to God will bring release from sin and set you on the road to recovery. Paul's message to Christians at Corinth was,

And such were some of you. But you were washed, but you were sanctified, but you were justified in the name of the Lord Jesus and by the Spirit of our God (1 Corinthians 6:11).

In the wake of failure of any kind, restoration is only possible if one can accept the grace of God and grasp the concept of repentance and forgiveness. Restoration is not possible if the person who has fallen into sin gives in to the temptation to pursue an immoral lifestyle. The only person God cannot forgive is the person who cannot believe in God's mercy and grace and will not repent of his sin. It is not God who has refused restoration; it is the one refusing to seek forgiveness. Likewise, restoration is only possible to one who is willing to accept the forgiveness of Christ that is freely available and redirect his energies into another area in the kingdom of God.

Grace is abundant and available for all types of moral sin. However, there are consequences associated with sin. Children born in an illicit relationship do not disappear when you repent. Diseases contacted and emotional traumas are not instantly healed when you receive the Holy Spirit. God does not erase your memory and fill your mind with pleasant thoughts of the past pain.

In some organizations ministers who experience moral failure are disqualified from holding license. This underscores the seriousness of immoral conduct in the life of a minister. While we believe in forgiveness and preach restoration, there are some ministries that will be negated in the fallout from moral failure. In this case a minister must seek a new occupation; sometimes he must train for a different vocation altogether. He may find restoration and the opportunity to minister in a new area, but the scars of his failure will be felt throughout life.

A youth pastor that falls into sexual sin with a minor may never have the opportunity to work with youth in the same capacity as before. However, this does not relieve him of the call to help others find their way to Christ or dismiss him from a ministry to youth. He may have to revise his approach. The experience and lesson he learned may be a valuable platform on which he could launch a book or move into the administration of the program, rather than working directly with youth. He may be doing a different job, but he can still find an outlet for the call God placed on his life.

Failure does not have to be final. Many times when one in ministry commits a sexual sin the outcome is total failure resulting in turning away from God altogether. When one chooses to abandon his commitment to God and no longer seeks to follow Christ, defeat is inevitable. However, God will never refuse one who truly repents of

> **Moral failure does not have to be mortal failure.**

wrong and surrenders his life to God. *There is hope for you!* The failure may disqualify you from holding a ministerial license with an organization; it may prevent you from working with a particular church or group, but the sin of immorality need not disqualify you from everlasting life. Moral failure does not have to be mortal failure.

The fallen can be restored to a relationship with Christ. John said, "If we confess our sins, He is faithful and just to forgive us *our* sins and to cleanse us from all unrighteousness" (1 John 1:9). This passage is often quoted to the unbeliever to offer them hope of forgiveness and salvation. The letter was originally written to believers, some of whom walked with the Lord but had fallen into sin along the way. John goes on to exhort the believers not to sin, but to remind them, "If anyone sins, we have an advocate with the Father, Jesus Christ the righteous" (1 John 2:1).

There must be a clear severance from sin, forsake the impure acts of the flesh and spirit. Paul wrote to Timothy:

> *Flee also youthful lusts;* but *pursue righteousness, faith, love, peace* with those who call on the Lord out of a pure heart (2 Timothy 2:22).

On the positive side of this verse is the instruction to pursue righteousness, faith, love, and peace. Active restoration requires initiating some positive actions. Just as you might tell an unbeliever, "Being a Christian is more than what you stop doing, but what you start doing!" The same is true for the believer who is seeking restoration. One who has fallen must take some proactive steps to make the transition from immoral conduct back to restored relationship with God.

Following are some positive steps one can initiate to embrace the process of restoration:

- Abandon the behavior that has brought defeat in your life.

- Separate yourself from places and people that caused you to succumb to temptation.

- Seek and receive forgiveness of sins and renewal of the Holy Spirit in your life.

- Practice positive character habits. Pursue righteousness, faith, love, and peace.

- Establish accountability to prevent further failure. The conclusion of the verse above says, *"... with those who call on the Lord out of a pure heart."* Your ability to pursue the positive is related to your network with others who seek purity in their lives.

- Submit to a spiritual authority in your life. You cannot be saved without a pastor, someone to watch for your soul.

- Seek to find a new outlet for ministry as you focus on other's needs rather than your own failures.

- Become a living example of God's grace!

In a previous book, I wrote, "If you haven't always been faithful to the calling of Christ, don't be too hard on yourself. Grace understands our fears and failures and still forgives."[26] *You will find that His grace is still amazing!*

---

[26] For more on the study of grace see the author's book: *Grace is a Pentecostal Message,* Terry R. Baughman, (Pleasanton, CA: Baughman Group Ministries, 2002).

8

Money and the Ministry

For the love of money is a root of all *kinds of* evil,
for which some have strayed from the faith in their
greediness, and pierced themselves through with many
sorrows. But you, O man of God, flee these things and
pursue righteousness, godliness, faith,
love, patience, gentleness.
—1 Timothy 6:10-11

Personal finance is an area of vital importance. A lack of integrity regarding financial responsibility holds the potential for lasting reproach on Christianity, the church, and the ministry. Concerning the reputation of preachers being irresponsible with money management, Joe Trull and James Carter wrote, "So notorious have clergy often been in financial mismanagement that in some financial circles people are warned against lending money to the professions that begin with "P": *plumbers, painters, prostitutes, and preachers."*[27]

While there are many conscientious and honest members of the clergy, there have been enough failures on this score to warrant such a dismal reputation. Writing on the subject of *The Minister's Finances,* Jesse Williams said, "The failure of one brings reproach upon many."[28]

It is true that people tend to remember the negative much longer than the positive. However, let us restate that quote as a challenge to live by: *the responsible financial stewardship of one brings respect upon many.* While we cannot speak nor act for all ministers, we can embrace an ethical standard in our own financial conduct that will be an example for others to follow.

Planning a budget requires discipline. The ability to live within the budget and balance the checkbook is an indispensable skill that must be developed and observed. While some personality temperament types enjoy organizing and the minutia of details, others would do just about anything to avoid bookkeeping and budgets. However, good financial stewardship requires that we all develop some abilities in this important area.

---

[27] Trull & Carter, *Ministerial Ethics,* 77.

[28] Jesse Williams, "The Minister's Finances" in *The Pentecostal Minister,* edited by J.L. Hall and David K. Bernard (Word Aflame Press, 1991), 67.

Recompense to no man evil for evil. *Provide things honest in the sight of all men* (Romans 12:17 KJV).

Guidelines for Success in Finances

1. Plan a Budget and Live by It

Detail income and expenses as much as possible. If you pastor a small church where the income is volatile, set yourself a conservative salary. As residual funds increase to a more appropriate level you can adjust your salary accordingly.

In the budget you can plan for the known monthly (or quarterly, etc.) expenses. Also plan for unexpected emergencies by including an undesignated amount in the budget that you can allocate when a special need arises. Planning ahead will help you avoid unnecessary debt.

Sound Christian financial advice is available from *Crown Financial Ministries* at www.crown.org (formerly known as *Christian Financial Concepts*). This organization exists to provide financial guidance in everything, from helping to plan a budget to setting up a living trust. They incorporate biblical principles and God-honoring ethics in all matters of financial stewardship.

2. Keep Good Records.

It is imperative to keep good financial records, both personally and for the church. Being consistent with record keeping has its advantages at tax time. You will have an accurate account of expenses and income. This will not only give you a clear conscience when declaring deductible expenses, but will also provide a tax savings by giving you evidence to claim allowable tax deductions, such as the business use of your vehicles when supported with a mileage record.

Keep informed of tax changes. There is a helpful tax advantage provided for ministers through a housing allowance. It should be set up properly to enjoy the benefit without fear of violation of the IRS code. There are bylaws and resolutions for expense reimbursement that need to be approved by the church (or church officers) in order to take full advantage of these provisions.

Aubrey Jayroe, a CPA and pastor, publishes an annual *Clergy & Church Tax Guide* to assist the minister and church staff to comply with IRS tax regulations. It is updated annually to keep up with current changes in the tax code.[29]

Another helpful resource is David Bernard's *Growing a Church, Seven Apostolic Principles*. In *Appendix A–Organizing a Church Legally*, he provides instruction for setting up bylaws in the new church plant that will provide needed non-taxable benefits to the pastor.[30]

3. Guard against Debt

Accumulation of debt will prohibit you from being free to respond to some opportunities the Lord will open

---

[29] Aubrey Jayroe, *Clergy & Church Tax Guide.* Available from PentecostalPublishing.com, Hazelwood, MO.

[30] David K. Bernard, *Growing a Church, Seven Apostolic Principles: A guide to evangelism and discipleship for pastors and workers in churches of every size*, (Hazelwood, MO: Word Aflame Press, 2001), 243-255.

for you. Personal debt is taken into consideration when one applies for the foreign missions field, as well as for home missions assistance to start a new church plant. If you have demonstrated irresponsibility in areas of finance no one wants to invest in your future financial failure!

Interest on debt is a robber of finance. Whatever benefits that may be gained by purchasing something on credit are quickly negated by accruing finance charges. Small minimum monthly payments on revolving credit  accounts are designed to keep you in debt and on a payment cycle the rest of your life. Slavery may be illegal but the trade is active in the credit card industry!

The rich rules over the poor, And *the borrower is servant to the lender* (Proverbs 22:7).

People at younger ages than ever before are carrying greater debt on credit cards. When I was a senior in college I was approved for my first Visa card (BankAmericard, at that time). I think it had a $300 limit! We now have young people coming to college *with* credit cards, having higher limits, and already maxed out! Often students are unable to come to college, or have to leave prematurely, because of high credit card payments. *We need some plastic surgery!*

It is not a sin to borrow, but care should be used to borrow only for appreciable items. Much is said in Scripture about good stewardship and responsibility in the area of finance. Ministers must set a good example to the members in their congregation in financial stewardship.

4. Resist Extravagant Lifestyles

Pastors and ministers should be able to live in nice houses and drive good cars when financially possible. However, attention should be given to avoid the appearance of opulence. You are in the public eye. Conservatism is always fashionable for the minister.

A good guideline is to live approximately at the *average* level of the *upper half* of your congregation. The car you drive should not embarrass people either by being a broken down rattletrap or a luxury limo. The neighborhood you live in should be as safe as possible for your family and respectable enough that you could invite anyone from your congregation to visit without shame. Of course, a mansion surrounded by a vast estate with a private golf course might give the impression of extravagance. The key here is balance. You should live according to your means, but not in excess. You should reflect integrity in wise investments for your future, without appearing to be selfishly hording the resources available to you.

If the people you serve are taking good care of you financially, they want to see you live within your means, neither above it nor below it. It is a delicate balance. Some will never begrudge you for having nice things, while others will always be critical of what you drive, where you live, or what you eat. As long as you know you are making conscientious decisions and living within your means don't be discouraged by the negative comments of others.

5. Be an Example in Giving

If we are responsible and honor God with our income, others will be inspired to do the same. If we tithe, others will be encouraged to give God the tenth. When we give to special needs, our membership will desire to become financially secure so they too will have enough resources to give when special needs are presented to the church.

The minister, of all people, should be consistent in the giving of tithes and offerings. The blessings of the Lord are contingent upon your faithfulness to this biblical principle:

> *Give, and it will be given to you:* good measure, pressed down, shaken together, and running over will be put into your bosom. *For with the same measure that you use, it will be measured back to you* (Luke 6:38).

According to this verse, God will use the same measure to give back to us what we are using to give to others and to His kingdom. If you use a teaspoon when you give, God will use a teaspoon to pour out blessings in your life. If you use barrels to bless others you can expect blessings by the barrel-full when God pours out your reward.

Cooperate freely and faithfully with your ministerial organization's financial plan. Each district (or state) in the organization has an established financial plan that has been approved by the ministers of that locale. It is the accepted method of financing the organization's operations. On the national level there is a required budget amount that may be paid annually or quarterly. When you become a part of an organization, you agree to the financial plan in effect. Honor it and you will be blessed!

Conducting the Business of the Lord

We live in a democracy. Sometimes people feel that the church should be governed democratically. While there are occasions to take a vote, as in the purchase of property or decisions requiring the majority sentiment, there are other times when a pastor must make decisions arbitrarily. When the decision concerns the spiritual well-being of the congregation a pastor must make the right decision even if it is unpopular and would never be approved if it depended on a vote.

At the other end of the spectrum from a democracy is an autocracy. This is a dictatorial system of rule, where tyrants and dictators govern according to their own selfish whims. There is no place for this kind of pastoring. This is where a pastor exercises supreme control and no one is allowed a voice in the affairs of the church and no explanation is given. Blind obedience is expected. This leads to *Jim Jones* and *David Koresh* type situations where the masses are deceived and lives are destroyed.

There is a balance between Laodicea (*laity-ruled*) and being a "lord over God's heritage" (1 Peter 5:3 KJV). God's desire is for a theocratic leadership, where God's man provides godly leadership and seeks God's direction for the church. This kind of leader knows that he must give an account to the Chief Shepherd and pastors with that accountability foremost in his mind.

Obey those who rule over you, and be submissive, for *they watch out for your souls, as those who must give account.* Let them do so with joy and not with grief, for that would be unprofitable for you (Hebrews 13:17).

Therefore *take heed to yourselves and to all the flock,* among which the Holy Spirit has made you overseers, to *shepherd the church of God* which He purchased with His own blood (Acts 20:28).

The pastor is the overseer of the Church. This is a divine appointment. If he is the overseer of the spiritual well being of the church, he must also be responsible in areas of fiscal responsibility and other areas of church administration. In this role he is a steward or a manager of that which has been entrusted into his care.

For a bishop must be blameless, *as a steward of God*, not self-willed, not quick-tempered, not given to wine, not violent, not greedy for money (Titus 1:7).

The growing church in the early pages of the Book of Acts had become burdensome in its administration within a very short time. Astounding revival results had produced headaches of organization and discipleship. Can you imagine a revival when 3,000 are converted the first day and 5,000 more in the following week? The Apostles in the early church were overwhelmed with the tasks of leadership and delegated some of the administrative responsibilities to those who had proven themselves to be _of good reputation._

> Then the twelve summoned the multitude of the disciples and said, "It is not desirable that we should leave the word of God and serve tables. Therefore, brethren, _seek out from among you seven men of good reputation, full of the Holy Spirit and wisdom, whom we may appoint over this business;_ but we will give ourselves continually to prayer and to the ministry of the word (Acts 6:2-4).

Good men and women can help share the administrative load in the church. It is not meant to be borne by the pastor alone. It is vital that you seek out those who are Spirit-filled and have gifts in the area of administration and finance. Too often carnal treasurers have wreaked havoc and stirred up strife in churches where this pattern was not followed. Loyal and responsible assistants are required for these important roles in the local church.

When there is a failing in a church organization the pastor is always held responsible in the public eye and also in many areas of financial responsibility. It is vital that the pastor not only be accountable himself but that he also _requires_ accountability on the part of those over which he has supervision. Accurate bookkeeping and responsible accounting are essential in the operation of the church.

The suggested system of local church government offered in the manual for _United Pentecostal Churches_ provides for pastoral authority in the following statement, "He shall have the oversight and superintendence of all interest of the church and all departments of its work, both spiritual and temporal" (Article III, Section 6).

With privilege comes responsibility. When you have a position of trust and leadership in the church there is greater responsibility. In a case of financial irresponsibility, the creditors will not come seeking the occasional visitor or the nominal member, but board members, church administration leaders, and especially the pastor!

Some practical guidelines for good financial leadership and accountability in the local church are as follows:

- The pastor should review all purchases and expenditures. In a larger church much can be delegated to an administrator or church leader, but the pastor should always give final approval for larger purchases over a fixed dollar amount. He must be aware of how money is being spent and how the records are being kept.

- Recognition of contributions and a letter of appreciation for support should be given periodically, from quarterly to annually. This provides an opportunity to thank the donors, and also supplies a friendly reminder that you notice if they are dropping off in their giving!

- An annual business meeting must be conducted to comply with state laws of incorporation. People are more inclined to support when they feel that the accounting is honest and the finance is being well-managed.

When you follow good accounting practices and financial responsibility, you are promised the blessing of the Lord and good will from the people that you pastor.

His lord said to him, "Well _done_, good and faithful servant; _you have been faithful over a few things, I will make you ruler over many things._ Enter into the joy of your lord" (Matthew 25:23).

9

Ministerial Relationships

*Finally, all of you, live in harmony with one another;
be sympathetic, love as brothers, be compassionate and
humble. Do not repay evil with evil or insult with
insult, but with blessing, because to this you were called
so that you may inherit a blessing.*
—1 Peter 3:8-9

Lawyers, doctors, and other professionals are taught
to observe a *code of ethics*. Those who do not abide
by these guidelines may be disciplined or expelled
by their profession. The ministry has a code of ethics as
well. Although, much of it may be an unwritten code, you
can still feel the effect of its violation even without formal
disciplinary action. Though you may be forgiven of some
infractions, continual violations will cause you to feel
ostracized by the ministry and segregated from fellowship.

There are written bylaws affecting some areas of
ministerial ethics, such as building a church near another

of your faith without permission. The written code requires you to make application to the district board and obtain the consent of the surrounding pastors. The unwritten ethic is to treat the neighboring churches with the respect that you would want to be given. Ethical conduct will win the goodwill of the local area pastors and cultivate respect and cooperation with each of them.

The following *Code of Ethics* was adopted by the United Pentecostal Church International at its General Conference in 1964. It was presented as being "not laws to govern but principles to guide."

My Code of Ethics[31]

*Striving to be a good minister of
the Lord Jesus Christ,
I will constantly prepare myself in body,
mind, and spirit,
I will safeguard the good name of the ministry;
[I will] speak the truth in love, live honestly,
and avoid embarrassing debts.
I will hold as sacred all confidences
shared with me.
I will exercise the authority of a spiritual leader
rather than that of a dictator.
I will seek to minister rather than to be
ministered unto, placing service above salary
and personal recognition,*

---

[31] "My Code of Ethics," *Position Papers*, Manual of the *United Pentecostal Church International* 2005, Hazelwood, MO, 152.

*and the unity and welfare of the church above
my own personal welfare.
I will seek to lead my church to accept its full
responsibility for community
and world service.
I will seek to build my church without
discrediting other churches,
soliciting members therefrom,
or casting reflection on other ministers.
I will not compete with another minister for a
call to a pastorate in an unethical manner.
I will, with my resignation, sever my pastoral
relations with any former parishioner
and will not make pastoral contacts in the field
of another pastor without his knowledge
and consent.
I will not accept the pastorate of a United
Pentecostal Church unless I am in accord with
the Articles of Faith and Constitution of the
general church body.
Having accepted a pastorate, I will not use my
influence to alienate the church or any portion
thereof from the fellowship or support of the
United Pentecostal Church.
If my convictions change,
I will be honorable enough to withdraw.*

This code of ethics would not be needed if all would treat each other "with brotherly love, in honor giving preference to one another" (Romans 12:10). When a person truly exhibits the love of Christ they will display his humility and ethics. Peter's admonition strikes at the heart of this issue.

> Finally, all of you be of one mind, having compassion for one another; *love as brothers,* be tenderhearted, be courteous (1 Peter 3:8).

Transferring Members

In any church there will be times when members become dissatisfied with something or someone in the congregation. It may be a situation where someone has said something hurtful, the pastor has made an unpopular decision, or sin has caused them to be disqualified in a particular ministry involvement. Whenever someone becomes unhappy with the church family, this may lead to a desire to change membership to another congregation.

The Scripture warns, "Offenses will come" (Luke 17:1 KJV). Everyone will have an occasion or an opportunity to be offended and to become bitter toward another. It is important that issues be worked through and conflicts resolved. Reconciliation is hampered if wounded members flee from the congregation and affiliate with another church. For this reason a pastor who receives a visit from members of another church should not welcome them to join his congregation, but encourage them to return to their former church, and resolve the issues. If the visiting members have a problem with their other pastor, it is very likely they eventually will have a problem with you.

There are occasions when a pastor will recommend a church transfer for a member due to irresolvable conflicts. For example, if a husband has been sexually involved with another member of the congregation, but repents, and is reconciled with his wife, it may be best for the couple to go elsewhere to church. This will provide an opportunity to work on rebuilding their marriage rather than confronting the *other* party in every service. In this situation the pastor of the couple should communicate with the pastor of the church where the couple desires to worship.

Communications and Christianity

Communication between pastors is vital to good ministerial relationships and maintaining ethical integrity. A lack of communication contributes to misunderstandings and speculation. It is possible to imagine all kinds of motives, attitudes, and intentions when you do not discuss relevant issues with the pastor involved. It is often easier to talk with others *about someone* rather than actually going to talk *to the one* with whom you have a misunderstanding. The problem is, talking *about someone* becomes gossip and does nothing to resolve the conflict. Pick up the phone, make an appointment, take the other minister to lunch and resolve the issue before it becomes a bigger problem.

In all communications a pastor should learn and observe basic etiquette. Whether it is using the home or office phones, cell phones, teleconference, or email, respect should be demonstrated for those with whom you are communicating. When making calls, each person should value the other's time as if it were as important as his own.

When a pastor receives a message on the answering machine or voice mail, he should return the call *as soon as possible*. The recorded message often makes that promise! Yet, I have heard many remark how poorly the response is when leaving messages for pastors. Pastors are busy, but they should never be too busy to politely return calls. The mark of an organized, efficient pastor is one who returns calls promptly.

Business executives would have difficulty succeeding if they were negligent in returning calls from clients. If an executive does not return his calls, it is safe to assume he is negligent in other areas of business. The ministry should not have this kind of reputation. If we desire the reputation of an organized and efficient church, it begins with the leadership practicing punctuality.

When a minister or pastor asks his secretary to make calls, it should be with the understanding that she follows through on the conversation and acquires the needed information for your convenience. It is never good to ask her to secure another minister on the line before putting the call through to you. This implies that your time is more valuable than the minister you are calling. It would be better for you to wait and make the call when you have time to do so. Some secular executives play this game to prove to others that they are more important. In reality, if a minister participates in this kind of action, it shows a lack of respect for a fellow minister.

As ministers, our relationships with other ministers of the gospel should be most important to us. Sometimes we are more conscientious toward the sinner and stranger than those of the fellowship. It is like we know what the world expects of us as Christians so we feel obligated to live up to that expectation. However, because another is a brother in the church, he is exempt from such treatment. We may see the need to be a good witness to the unbeliever, but feel our Christian sister should understand if we are rude or uncaring. Conversely, the Scriptures instruct that there should be exemplary treatment of the church family. Notice Paul's words of admonition:

> Therefore, as we have opportunity, let us do good to all, *especially to those who are of the household of faith* (Galatians 6:10).

> Let nothing be done through selfish ambition or conceit, but in lowliness of mind let each *esteem others better than himself.* Let each of you look out not only for his own interests, but also for *the interests of others* (Philippians 2:3-4).

If we will follow the instructions of Scripture we will have good and healthy relationships with others both within and outside the church body. Everyone responds to love and respect. When we genuinely respect others we will receive the same in return.

Fellowship

The opportunity for fellowship comes from among those who share your burden and calling. Some of the best comradeship you will ever enjoy will be in fellowship with other preachers, those of similar calling. Cultivate good relationships with other ministers and their families. The rewards are personally enriching.

There is an invisible distinction between the church member and minister that makes this level of camaraderie impossible within the local congregation. While you may enjoy wonderful times of fellowship with members of your congregation, you will be unable to share some of your feelings and frustrations with them.

Ministers' Retreats or special conferences designed for the ministry are especially attractive to the preacher. It is in these meetings he can *let his hair down* and be more vulnerable to others who share his burden and challenges. When ministers are able to share their hearts there is a bond of affection that will bless the soul.

Ministerial fellowship does not have to be planned retreats or greatly organized events. It can take place as easily as inviting a neighboring pastor to meet at a favorite restaurant or inviting a minister to share a day trip for sight-seeing or shopping. Some ministers enjoy a round of golf or a fishing trip. Making friends is natural when you find a hobby or pastime that is mutually enjoyed and willingly shared.

Times of fellowship should not be reduced to gossip or gripe sessions about your church members or other pastors. Care should be taken that these times of fellowship are encouraging and positive events. You will be able to lift the spirits of another when you focus on positive conversation. Likewise, when you need encouragement someone else will be able to lift your spirits if you have developed this type of relationship with your fellow ministers.

Paul wrote to the Corinthians that they would submit to the ministry of Stephanas and "everyone who works and labors with us." He commended their ministry and said "they refreshed my spirit" (1 Corinthians 16:15-18). Every minister needs the ministry of someone else. Fellowship, friendship, and encouragement are essential aspects of a healthy ministry.

Apparently there was some discussion among the Corinthians over whose ministry they were converted under. Some identified with Apollos, others with Paul. Paul rebuked them as being carnal. He said that we are just "ministers through whom you believed ... I planted, Apollos watered, but God gave the increase" (1 Corinthians 3:4-7). Paul saw his work as being integrated with that of Apollos and other ministers. He said, "We are God's fellow workers" (vs. 9).

If we can see the ministry as a team, and that we are all on the team with God, there will be less self-promotion among us. We will not be so concerned over who gets the credit for church growth statistics, the number of baptisms, or how many received the Holy Spirit. As an evangelist, if hundreds receive the Spirit under your preaching, *to God be the glory!* That only indicates that someone else has been witnessing, teaching Bible studies, and preparing believers for the entrance of the Spirit in their lives. It is not a cause for arrogance or a feeling that people cannot receive the Spirit unless you are there to preach!

The talents and gifts of individuals are as unique as snowflakes. Each one has a special role to play in the kingdom of God. Likewise, in the ministry no two are alike. God has enabled every minister to fulfill a special task. The callings are as diverse as the prophet Jeremiah, the disciple Thomas, and the apostle Peter, but God has a place of ministry for each one. You must not impose your calling on your contemporaries. If prison ministry is your passion, don't insist that everyone share your zeal. If teaching home Bible studies is your mantra, *sing it,* just don't expect everyone else to sing in unison. Whatever ministry, calling, or passion you have been called to do, fulfill your responsibility and recognize that God has a unique plan for others as well.

Tolerance

Admittedly, you will not always have a wonderful relationship with every other minister. God has made such glorious diversity in humanity (and in the ministry) that we will forever find that some people just do not see things our way! This is a wonderful opportunity to practice *tolerance* for those who have a different viewpoint.

Tolerance has been given a bad name in recent culture. It has become the buzzword of acceptability. Tolerance is preached by a liberal press to promote every immoral practice and illicit act. Tolerance is freely applied to every liberal idea, and then totally abandoned when conservative values are expressed. When other philosophies and esoteric religious practices are promoted, we are expected to embrace them with *tolerance,* but when the life changing Gospel is proclaimed, it is quickly condemned as being *intolerant.*

That being said, there is a need for tolerance in Christianity. Tolerance is simply the capacity for recognizing and *respecting* the beliefs and practices of others. While the truth of Scripture makes some exclusive claims that cannot be compromised, we can still *respect* another's viewpoint. Sometimes in our zeal for *the Truth* we tend to lump all of our opinions and assumptions in the same irrefutable philosophical package. While one may be dogmatic in defense of baptism, one cannot be so certain in a particular understanding of prophecy. Here is an area for the exercise of tolerance. We can respect our fellow minister's view concerning the *seven trumpets,* even if we disagree with his interpretation.

Rather than respectfully discussing the disparity, many are prone to alienate and avoid those with whom they have differences. Worse yet, some will ridicule and demean the character of one with which they have had disagreements. This is unchristian and unacceptable behavior for a minister of the gospel. If ministers portray this type of behavior toward one another, sowing the seeds of division with a brother, what kind of behavior can we expect to harvest in our congregations?

A minister may feel strongly concerning particular views in his personal disciplines. It is the prerogative of the minister to teach these areas of commitment to his local congregation. If he truly feels that wearing a *top hat* will make men more spiritual, he can teach that as a doctrine. However, the minister should not expect the entire

185

organization to adopt his view. Neither should he impose his personal view in public forums where members of other congregations are present. If it is a *personal conviction*, it is just that, personal, and should not be imposed on others. If it is a biblical doctrine, then he is free to teach it from a correct interpretation of the Word of God and let other ministers judge the validity of his application of biblical truth.

Personal convictions, if they truly are, will bear the scrutiny of friendly discussions. With respect and tolerance we can express our opinions and listen to other viewpoints. When the discussion is over, if neither are convinced of opposing views, we can disagree *without being disagreeable.*

Is it possible to disagree and still be friends? I believe it is. I have good friends that would not agree with me on every point. *It is okay if they want to be wrong!* Actually, there are some areas which we have discussed and know that we are not in agreement. We now tend to avoid those areas of discussion. We have agreed to disagree. Now we share fellowship, discuss other issues, and sometimes we will still disagree, because we are individuals with our own opinions. This does not prevent us from being friends, sharing a meal, or even going on a short vacation together.

Tolerance is a two-way street. It is easy to expect others to show tolerance for our views, but we may not show the same respect to them. The *golden rule* still applies. If we want to be respected, we must show respect. If we wish to receive tolerance, we must practice tolerance.

Paul taught us to show respect for a brother that is offended by our liberties. The scriptural example was *food.* It seems that because of the cultural prevalence of offering food to idols, this became a real source of contention among believers in the early church. Should one eat food that was previously offered to idols? While today this controversy seems frivolous, it was so important in the first century that the council in Jerusalem included "that you abstain from things offered to idols" in their prohibition passed on to Gentile believers (Acts 15:28-29). It is listed in the context right along with "sexual immorality."

Paul wrote to the Romans and addressed the issue of judging a brother or offending the faith of another:

> Therefore let us pursue the things which make for peace and the things by which one may edify another. *Do not destroy the work of God for the sake of food.* All things indeed are pure, but it is evil for the man who eats with offense.
>
> It is good neither to eat meat nor drink wine *nor do anything by which your brother stumbles or is offended or is made weak* (Romans 14: 19-21).

Some traditions that you observe may only serve to prevent offense. Even that motivation is commended in Scripture. Paul addresses the subject of idols and food again in 1 Corinthians 8:4-13. He sums up the passage saying, "If food makes my brother stumble, I will never again eat meat, lest I make my brother stumble" (vs. 13). He did not

187

accept the position that some foods make us better or worse, but for the sake of maintaining good fellowship, one should avoid offending a weaker brother.

> But food does not commend us to God; for neither if we eat are we the better, nor if we do not eat are we the worse. But *beware lest somehow this liberty of yours become a stumbling block to those who are weak* (1 Corinthians 8:8-9).

The burden of avoiding offense does not rely solely on one; the *offended* and the *offender* are commanded to love one another. Jesus said, "By this all will know that you are My disciples, *if you have love for one another"* (John 13:35). So the key for tolerance is love. When we love as Christ loved we become more longsuffering. Longsuffering is another word for tolerance. Our various views and distinctive differences would be minimized if we truly loved one another.

Thomas À Kempis, a medieval Christian monk in Germany wrote in the *Imitation of Christ:*

> *"In things essential, unity;*
> *in doubtful, liberty;*
> *in all things, charity."*

This concept of tolerance is embodied in the *fundamental doctrine* of the United Pentecostal Church International. It is emphasized in the second paragraph after the brief statement of doctrine as follows:

The basic and fundamental doctrine of this organization shall be the Bible standard of full salvation, which is repentance, baptism in water by immersion in the name of the Lord Jesus Christ for the remission of sins, and the baptism of the Holy Ghost with the initial sign of speaking with other tongues as the Spirit gives utterance.

We shall endeavor to keep the unity of the Spirit until we all come into the unity of the faith, at the same time admonishing all brethren that they shall not contend for their different views to the disunity of the body.

In this organization, members are encouraged to focus on unifying characteristics rather than the things that divide. Practice tolerance rather than division. That is what keeps us *united*.

Selfishness

Selfishness will cause a man to withdraw from fellowship and become a loner. He begins to dwell on infractions and hurts in the past rather than all the positive interaction with friends. When a brother feels violated, the resentment builds as the deed escalates in his mind. Soon, he is so full of self-inflicted pain, he withdraws and cuts himself off from others, afraid to open up to more hurt. Resentment festers in the humid swamp of selfishness, a perfect environment to cultivate the destructive bacteria of bitterness; and bitterness, when carried by unbridled thoughts, injects its fatal disease into the soul.

189

Unfortunately, one offense can cause many casualties, the loss of good friends unrelated to the circumstances. If a man can cleanse himself of selfishness, resentment has no place to flourish. He no longer sees himself as the victim. He understands the Scripture "all things work together for good" (Romans 8:28) and allows hurtful situations to build character rather than destroy relationships.

Selfishness is a thief. It robs us of faith and replaces it with fear; it robs us of forgiveness and substitutes it with bitterness. Selfishness robs us of confidence and trades it for intimidation; it robs us of humility and replaces it with pride. All these things track back to selfishness.

> Ministry has the potential of extending its influence beyond the limitations of life.

Ministry has the potential of extending its influence beyond the limitations of life. It is the opportunity to do something truly significant with your life that has an eternal value. If your work is self-centered it will perish with you. There will be no lasting reward for your accomplishments. Jesus spoke of the hypocrites who performed their religious acts "to be seen by men." He said, "They have their reward" (Matthew 6:5). The limited glory they receive from the accolades of others is all the reward they will get for their selfish acts of piety.

Many pastors of churches and leaders of organizations have built good works that were not

190

anchored in Jesus Christ. When the pastor moved on, the church eventually dissolved; when the founder passed, the organization declined. We must forever point our followers to Jesus Christ. He is the only eternal One. He is the cornerstone of our foundation. Only a ministry built on His foundation will stand the test of time. A self-centered structure is doomed to fall. *If a man's work will not stand the test of time, how will it ever bear the scrutiny of eternity?*

Cross-Denominational Relationships

In the ministerial community you will have contacts on occasions with member of the clergy from other denominations. As a church grows in influence and through evangelistic endeavors new members will be attracted that have been members of some of these denominational churches. Do we have an ethical obligation to the ministers of other denominations?

Some increase in membership will occur as members of other denominations are persuaded of the tenets of faith represented by your church. This conversion may come through their search for more understanding, joining a Bible study group, receiving a new spiritual experience, or due to the evangelistic outreach of your church. As you rejoice in their spiritual growth and the addition of members to the congregation, it may not occur to you to even consider the church the new member previously attended.

Most commonly, we have considered members of other denominational churches fair game for outreach. Though they may have previously experienced a conversion through repentance, or even been baptized as church members, the full gospel message promises something that many denominational church members have not experienced. The importance of receiving the gift of the Holy Spirit and water baptism in Jesus' name becomes paramount. Church membership is seldom considered. New converts are not required to change churches, but few will consider returning to their *former* formal church once they experience Spirit-filled worship and the vibrant preaching of anointed messages that they now crave.

While we are convinced of the vital truth of our doctrine, we must consider our potential relationship with the pastors or leaders of congregations that are suffering loss in their membership. While our response in this situation would be different than if we had visitors from a church of our faith, there needs to be some thought as to how we would handle this situation. Perhaps a card or letter to the pastor or minister of the former church would be appropriate. It should be worded in such a way as not to *gloat* over your new convert, but to acknowledge that a former member has joined your congregation. You might open the door for communication by giving your personal phone number if he would like to discuss the transfer with you. The clergy member may be interested in knowing more about the experience his faithful member found that would cause him to change denominational loyalties.

Professional courtesy should be extended to a minister of any denomination for the following reasons:

- **Christian responsibility** - *"Do unto others as you would have them do unto you"* serves as our golden rule. Perhaps this will serve as a basis for our initial response. *"How would you like to be treated?"*

- **Respect for Position** - Understand that this man or woman is in a place of spiritual leadership in his or her congregation similar to our position. Everyone deserves respect. If we disrespect a church leader, what kind of feeling will he have toward us and our church?

- **Opportunity for Conversion** - We never know when we will have the opportunity to be like Aquila and Priscilla who showed the *"way more perfectly"* to the Alexandrian Jew, Apollos (Acts 18:24-26). He taught eloquently *and* mightily in the Scriptures, but only had knowledge of the baptism of John. Some of the greatest revivals in foreign countries have been among ministers of other denominations coming to experience the power of the Holy Spirit and seeing their need to be baptized (*or re-baptized*) in Jesus' name.

- **Demonstrate a Spirit of Cooperation** - In many areas there are ministerial associations in the city that local clergy members may join. This may provide opportunities for ministry to the poor and indigent of the community, cooperative evangelism, or other community projects. Each opportunity or request for involvement must be judged on its own merits. Though some events, such as a city-wide crusade for all denominations, are sometimes difficult, it should be the minister's desire to show himself friendly and cooperative, without compromising faith or yielding his convictions.

Being a Good Host

In pastoral ministry you will frequently have opportunity, even the necessity, to practice skills of hospitality. Paul included the ability to be *hospitable* in lists of ministerial qualification, both in 1 Timothy 3:2 and in Titus 1:8 (see page 95). In Romans, Paul said we must be "given to hospitality" (Romans 12:13). When Peter wrote about being stewards of God's grace, he said that we should, "*Be hospitable* to one another without grumbling" (1 Peter 4:9). Basically, he said *quit your grumbling and enjoy fellowship!*

The fine art of hospitality must be practiced to perfection in the ministry. Many occasions will necessitate the entertainment of guest speakers, missionaries, and evangelists. Other occasions will present themselves when it will be necessary to entertain church members who need extra attention or counseling. New converts or prospective members are often won as friends before they are won to God.

Among the critical qualities of ministers, the Scriptures give several admonitions concerning serving, giving, and entertaining hospitably. Who knows when you will even have the opportunity to entertain an angel!

Let brotherly love continue. Do not forget to
entertain strangers, for by so doing *some have
unwittingly entertained angels* (Hebrews 13:1-2).

A visiting minister that you are unacquainted with
may be initially reserved. There is a possibility that his
wife may feel apprehensive, as though they are "barging
in" on you, your family and your church. You can make
them feel wanted or unwanted by your initial reaction to
their presence. Greet them with a warm smile and a
friendly attitude. The pastor's wife can be very helpful in
this area. If you meet them for the first time just before
church, she can ask the evangelist's wife to sit with her.
This will make the guest feel more comfortable, especially
if she is a stranger to your church. If the evangelist's wife
has an infant or other young child, you may ask if she
needs someone to watch them while she participates on the
platform. If the pastor's wife does not feel comfortable
offering her services, she should find a kind person who
loves children to help out during services.[32]
The responsibility of taking care of an evangelist or
special speaker falls on your shoulders as the host. If you
are going to have a minister come while you are on
vacation or away for a weekend, appoint someone to be
the host to your guests taking them out to dinner or
making other arrangements. If you have an assistant, this is
a great opportunity for him to get acquainted with the

---

[32] Baughman, *Social Graces*, 372.

evangelist and his family. It also gives him some experience in the area of pastoral duties.

It helps to avoid misunderstandings when you communicate your plans to the visiting minister. Following are some questions you may need to ask as you anticipate the needs of your guest. By answering these questions up front, it will help make the initial visit more comfortable.

- Will you be dining with your guests?

- If they have a trailer or you have an evangelist quarters, do they prefer to eat there and have the church members provide groceries?

- Do you prefer to take them out for dinner and allow them to eat other meals in their facility?

- If they are in a hotel, have you taken the appropriate steps to make sure they are taken care of for the duration of the time they are ministering to your church?

- Are there any health issues that prevent them from eating conventional foods? Most evangelists will not make an issue out of their special dietary needs unless you ask.

If you communicate your desires to your guest speakers and evangelists, and in turn find out their needs and desires, the experience can be mutually beneficial, freeing the guest to focus more on his ministry and making the visit an enjoyable one.

Entertaining the Dinner Guest

One of our favorite pastimes is eating out. I'm not sure why we like to socialize around the table so much, but it seems to be the most obvious place to fellowship. Perhaps it is because we have Jesus as our example. He often had fellowship with His disciples while dining in someone's home. John 12:2 records that Jesus ate at the home of Lazarus, Mary and Martha. In Mark 2:16, He ate with the sinners and tax collectors. In Luke 7:36, He ate with a Pharisee. Jesus chose the dinner table to explain to His disciples the curse of betrayal and the hope of a new covenant. On other occasions, He was the host breaking bread for a crowd of five thousand hungry people at one time and four thousand at another (Mark 8:19-20).

One day soon Jesus will be our host. He has arranged the marriage supper of the Lamb for us when we get to Heaven (Revelation 19:9). Every dinner we attend, every time we sit down at the table and put on our best manners, we are practicing and preparing for the ultimate dinner invitation of our lives.

As a pastor, you will have many opportunities to be the host to friends, visiting ministers, and members of your congregation. You may enjoy the relaxing atmosphere of your home or treating them to your favorite fine-dining restaurant. Whatever you do, enjoy your guests to the fullest by choosing the environment you feel most comfortable in as a host.

Dining In

To invite your guests over for a home-cooked meal is a wonderful gesture. Making them feel at home is the most important element of hospitality. A guest can detect almost immediately if you are uncomfortable with people in your home. Company will feel only as comfortable as you are. They will relax if you are relaxed, and they will come back if you welcome them. Since the bulk of the responsibility of entertaining in the home falls on the lady of the house, it is imperative that she also feels comfortable with the arrangement.

Working a full-time job and preparing meals for an evangelist's family during revival can be quite stressful. Many pastor's wives solicit help from the ladies in their churches who enjoy contributing to the revival in this way. A woman with an unsaved husband may not be able to support the revival in offerings, but may view this as a wonderful opportunity to contribute.[33]

There is no need to feel pressured to host a formal dining experience each evening of a revival. If your wife has a nice table set with her favorite china one night and paper plates the next, the important thing is that you enjoy your guests.

If dining in your home is inconvenient during the week, you may want to save the invitation into your home for a time when you don't have to work the next day. If time will not allow you to serve your guests in the comfort of your home at all, eating out can be just as hospitable. Consider your wife in the decision. Dining out the entire

---

[33] Ibid, 374.

revival may be a better option if your wife is not comfortable inviting people into your home.

Dining Out

Dining out is gaining popularity in our fast-paced lives. It is convenient, fast, and requires no clean-up. For those reasons, evangelists and speakers are finding themselves eating out more often. Most guests will appreciate the effort you make to choose a favorite restaurant or dining somewhere that you reserve for special occasions. Your family will welcome special guests when they know it includes dining out at some special places—*especially your wife.*

When you invite a guest to go out, it is with the understanding that you are responsible for the ticket. If you do not plan to pay when a group of friends go out, and yet it is your idea, ask if they can join you in a *dutch treat.* If you want to treat them, make your intentions clear in the beginning. If your friends don't have money to go out, it may be that they will decline, not because they don't want to be with you, but because of limited finances.

If you are the host and will be paying for the meal, let your guests know what they can order. Make some suggestions on the menu so they will know what price range is acceptable. It is not good etiquette to allow your dinner guest to pay the tip. As the host, you are taking care of the entire bill, including the tip. If your guest insists, the most gracious thing to do is allow him the pleasure, avoiding a scene.

When dining with a group of ministers, it is a sign of respect to ask the eldest of the group to offer the prayer.

If there is a dignitary present, then the honor is given to him. When children are present, it is a good time to teach them respect for their elders, explaining that they can pray when it is just the family or very close friends.

10

Pastor & Member Relationships

Therefore, as we have opportunity,
let us do good to all, especially to those
who are of the household of faith.
—Galatians 6:10

Crucial to successful church leadership are the relationships between the pastor and congregation. The effectiveness and propriety which we maintain these relationships will contribute to our success. While we are at times *"all things to all men,"* there must ever be the awareness of distinction between leader and laity. Though we are not better than the people, we are not on the same level with the people. We will be held to a higher accountability because of our leadership position. *"For everyone to whom much is given, from him much will be required"* (Luke 12:48).

The pastor or church leader should avoid projecting an air of superiority. Rather than leading from a position of arrogance one should follow the leadership style of Jesus:

> But he who is *greatest* among you shall be your *servant* (Matthew 23:11).

> And *whoever desires to be first among you, let him be your slave;* just as the Son of Man did not come to be served, but to serve, and to give His life a ransom for many (Matthew 20:27-28).

Jesus cared for the widow; He compassionately touched the crippled, the blind, and welcomed little children to play at His feet. The example He gave us while walking the dusty roads of this life was that of a servant. He truly *ministered* to those around Him. He never expected to be seated at the head of the table nor given the best room in the house. He said He had no place to rest his head. He must have spent many nights sleeping out under the stars. He spent enough time walking among the people to get to know them and to find out what their needs were. Then, His next move was to offer hope, hope of healing, hope of deliverance, and hope of everlasting life. He was not too good to wash the feet of His disciples. By this act, He gently reminded them that He was the example, implying that they do the same. *The greatest in God's kingdom is the best servant!*

Assuredly, I say to you, among those born of women there has *not risen one greater than John the*

Baptist; but *he who is least* in the kingdom of heaven *is greater* than he (Matthew 11:11).

Although Jesus moved among those He ministered to, there was a certain distinction that kept Him separate. He was the amicable Master, the approachable Almighty. He was the King and the Servant in one body, showing us how to minister in the truest sense of the word. The minister's separation from the congregation should not be perceived as aloofness or arrogance. There should be an attitude of servanthood, a willingness to serve—to follow the example of Jesus.

From this position of service there must also be an assumed authority. This is the contradiction of roles best demonstrated by Jesus. A servant having authority!

For *He taught them as one having authority,* and not as the scribes (Matthew 7:29).

The confidence in your call and the Spirit within will confirm the authority of your spiritual leadership. When you speak or lead, others will recognize the authority you exhibit and willingly follow. If you lack spiritual authority you will never have enough ability to make people follow your leadership.

The pastor provides service to the members of his congregation. He is on call in the event of sickness, regardless of the hour. He is available when the children are born and will dedicate them to the Lord. He will perform baptisms, weddings, and funerals for the people that he pastors. He will be there when tragedy strikes, when there is a celebration, and when there is a need for counsel or comfort.

While the pastor may fish, golf, or hunt with members of the congregation, he should always remember his position of leadership and conduct himself in such a way as to foster their continued respect. Ethical behavior is a standard of conduct and moral judgment. If this is not a part of the minister's life at all times he will lose the confidence and respect of those he has been called to lead. A pastor sees every leisure activity as an opportunity to show Christ. He sees every dinner engagement as a chance to share the Word with others. As Jesus used different circumstances to teach His disciples, so the pastor uses every occasion with the members as quality time, shepherding them, loving them, and teaching them.

When a pastor resigns or a member of his congregation moves to another church, careful re-evaluation of your close relationships should be considered. Members have a sense of loyalty when they are under the leadership of a pastor for some time. This loyalty is difficult to re-direct to a new pastor, if the previous pastor keeps in frequent contact with them. It is never easy to sever relationships with people in your congregation when you feel God has called you to move to another area. But unfortunately, that is the most effective and ethical practice. At least for a time, while the congregation adjusts to a new shepherd, it is good to avoid contact and give them some space to re-establish loyalty to someone else. If members continue to contact you, reaffirm the new pastor and carefully detach yourself from any transitional conflicts. When the new pastor feels the time for settling in has transpired, he may give you the liberty of contacting someone in his congregation. You should never contact members of your former congregation without the pastor's knowledge and his approval.

On the other hand, if members of your congregation move to another area, it is best not to contact them after they are settled in a new church. Offer your support, help them find a new church, and contact the pastor where they choose to visit. When they find a new church to attend, encourage them to get to know the new pastor and look to him for guidance.

The First Lady

The pastor's wife is the *First Lady* of the church. On various occasions, different members of the congregation will honor her with special tribute. These gifts and recognitions are compliments to both her and her husband's leadership. The congregation should be allowed to treat her like the *First Lady* with no fear of jealousy on her husband's part. On the other hand, the pastor's wife should fill the role proudly and honorably. The pastor's wife does not only have the pastor to answer to, but she has a whole group of ladies to whom she is responsible.

Four Big "I's"

Both the pastor and his wife may be honored at times, but it should never be expected. Once it is, honor with the One who is most important is lost. Humility is the virtue that brings honor to God. There is an old saying, "There are no big *I's* or little *you's* in the kingdom of God." This is very true. The only big *I's* a pastor should seek after are:

- **Influence** – He should use his influence to lead the flock God has placed in his care. In doing so he has the awesome opportunity to impart the values that have been given him through the precious Word of God. The pastor will be an example for the congregation to follow.

- **Impact** – The pastor should seek to make an impact on every life he contacts. This is not, however, limited solely to the members of the congregation, but to all he meets on a daily basis. One should feel the challenge to touch the life of the bank teller, the postal clerk, or the cashier at the grocery store.

- **Impartiality** – It is imperative to show the same love and concern to each person in the congregation. Favoritism will cripple the leader's influence on the membership. It is a great challenge for a pastor's wife to be impartial, especially at times when she experiences loneliness. This is the time to seek out another pastor's wife in the district for friendship and encouragement.

- **Involvement** – The congregation measures support by involvement. The pastor and his wife should be involved in as many activities surrounding the church as possible. This cannot be done without a great measure of balance between personal involvement in the church and family responsibilities. As the church grows, the pastor or his wife may not be able to attend every social event sponsored by the church, but at the same time, they should not be absent so often that they become inaccessible. Being involved with the members of the church makes you accessible and available whenever you are needed.[34]

---

[34] Ibid, 381-382.

11

Pastor & Assistant Relationships

These things command and teach. Let no one despise
your youth, but be an example to the believers in word,
in conduct, in love, in spirit, in faith, in purity.
Till I come, give attention to reading, to exhortation,
to doctrine. Do not neglect the gift that is in you,
which was given to you by prophecy with the laying on
of the hands of the eldership. Meditate on these things;
give yourself entirely to them, that your progress may
be evident to all. Take heed to yourself and to the
doctrine. Continue in them, for in doing this you will
save both yourself and those who hear you.
—1 Timothy 4:11-16

L oyalty is the premium quality of the Assistant
Pastor. There is a scriptural principle of *sowing and
reaping* that you can depend on. If you are loyal and
faithful to your pastor and leaders, it will be rewarded
when you are in positions of leadership. God will allow

you to have those under you who will show you the same honor you have shown to others. As an assistant, purpose to do everything possible to make the job of the leader easier and support him in his responsibilities.

The *second man* or the assistant fills a valued role in ministry. A church can only grow so much under the leadership of one man. A successful pastor in Arizona once told me that a man can only pastor about fifty people. If the church is to grow larger, the pastor must delegate leadership responsibilities. He must allow someone to help him pastor in order to reach more people.

Moses learned early in his new pastoral leadership of Israel in the wilderness, that he could not possibly be the "pastor" or judge to this awesome host of people. His father-in-law, Jethro, shared some valuable wisdom that would empower Moses to become the effective leader that he was capable of becoming.

Jethro observed that Moses was wearied after spending the long day "from morning until evening" judging the people (Exodus 18:13). He said, "The thing that you do is not good" (vs. 17). He then offered the following advice:

> Both you and these people who are with *you will surely wear yourselves out.* For this thing *is* too much for you; *you are not able to perform it by yourself.* Listen now to my voice; I will give you counsel, and God will be with you: Stand before God for the people, so that you may bring the difficulties to God. And you shall teach them the statutes and the laws, and show them the way in

which they must walk and the work they must do.

Moreover _you shall select from all the people able men, such as fear God, men of truth, hating covetousness; and place such over them to be rulers of thousands, rulers of hundreds, rulers of fifties, and rulers of tens. And let them judge the people at all times._ Then it will be that every great matter they shall bring to you, _but every small matter they themselves shall judge._ So it will be easier for you, for they will bear the burden with you (Exodus 18:18-22).

Jethro convinced Moses that the way he was leading was too much for him. He then counseled Moses to (1) teach the people the statues and laws (so they could make some judgment on their own!), (2) select God-fearing men to be leaders. Some would be delegated as leaders over a thousand, while others would lead a hundred, fifty, or ten, and they would judge the small matters, and (3) only bring the big stuff to Moses!

Sometimes churches cannot grow because pastors want to be involved in every little decision in the church. Nothing can be decided without the pastor's permission or approval. It is important that the pastor be aware of what is going on in the church, but he must trust others to follow after God and make good decisions as well! If we want to see the church grow we must allow people to grow in their God-ordained gifts and become the leaders God designed them to be.

Sometimes we say the pastor is building a church, but in reality he is building people. The building is not the church. The people that worship in the building are the church. In an article for a *Christian Life College* journal, *Third Millennium Ministry*, I wrote, "Our emphasis should always be on people rather than properties, the person rather than the place. Often our goal in church planting is to "get a building," and the *church* becomes the structure."[35]

> **Our emphasis should always be on people rather than properties, the person rather than the place.**

When a pastor takes the time to mentor leaders in his congregation, he is building up the kingdom of God; he is building the church. When we view our work as a complement to the body of Christ and our congregation as just a small part of His *church,* then we will be less possessive about our assembly and more convinced that there is only *one church!*

The truth is—the church is bigger than any one of us. The church was here before we arrived and the church will be here long after we have gone on to our reward. It is our duty to allow the church to be the church and use people in their areas of ministry and giftedness.

---

[35] Terry R. Baughman, "Future Church" in *Third Millennium Ministry, Vol. 1,* (Stockton, CA: Christian Life College Press, 2004), 25.

Some associate pastors will always be assistants. They have found their area of giftedness and are using their talents to fulfill the work of the Lord. Every young minister is not destined to become a full-time pastor of a large church with many on the staff. There will be some, but the average size church in America is about 75 in attendance. There are a lot of small congregations needing pastors and assistants.

If it is your calling to be an assistant, fulfill the purpose of God in your life. Be the best assistant any pastor ever had. Rejoice in your calling!

If you are filling the role of assistant and long to be a pastor of your *own church,* be content where you are for the present. Be the best assistant you can be until the Lord opens doors for you to plant a church or to take an established work. In the meantime, while you are not responsible for the full operation of the church, learn all you can. Observe the people, learn from the pastor, seek God's wisdom, and let this time not be wasted while wishing you were somewhere else.

Faithful to Leadership

The relationship between Moses and the young man Joshua is a wonderful scriptural illustration of a pastor and his assistant. Even before Joshua was called the *assistant* of Moses he was faithful, a man of integrity, and a man that Moses could count on to get things done. In the first mention of Joshua, he was already recognized as a leader. He was given a job, "Choose your fighting men and fight our enemy, Amalek." In the simple statement,

"Joshua did as Moses said to him," there is the quality of faithfulness and dependability.

> And Moses said to Joshua, "*Choose us some men and go out*, fight with Amalek. Tomorrow I will stand on the top of the hill with the rod of God in my hand. *So Joshua did as Moses said to him*, and fought with Amalek. And Moses, Aaron, and Hur went up to the top of the hill (Exodus 17:9-10).

Chosen for Leadership

Apparently, Joshua continued to impress Moses with his loyal service. The next time he was mentioned in Exodus he had been promoted! Scripture records that it was Moses and *his assistant Joshua* that went up to the mountain of God (Exodus 24:13).

Joshua distinguished himself in his service to Moses, while many of the people were given over to idolatry in the worship of the golden calf. Joshua was not among the idolaters, but stayed as near to the mountain as possible.

When Moses was directed by God to leave the mountain to confront the idolatrous celebration, Joshua knew nothing of the sin among the people and mistook the frivolity for the sound of war.

And when Joshua heard the noise of the people as they shouted, he said to Moses, "*There is a noise of war in the camp.*" But he said: "*It is not the noise of the shout of victory, Nor the noise of the cry of defeat, But the sound of singing I hear."*

So it was, as soon as he came near the camp, that he saw the calf and the dancing. So Moses' anger became hot, and he cast the tablets out of his hands and broke them at the foot of the mountain (Exodus 32:17-19).

If an assistant will stay close to God and to the pastor, he will not become embroiled in issues that sometimes infiltrate the church. It is easy to become ensnared in a conflict among members and be pressured to take sides in a matter. If you can be persuaded to take an opposing side from the pastor, then there is the potential for division. People may try to use the assistant, assuring him that he would make a better pastor than the one they have, causing the church to be split. A wise assistant will keep clear of divisive issues and confide in the pastor to bring healing and restoration from conflict.

Loyalty to leadership will be rewarded in the future.

Loyalty to leadership will be rewarded in the future. Even in situations where you disagree with the pastoral leadership, it is wise to support him publicly and refuse to join in any opposition to the church leadership. The time will come when some will oppose you, and you will be grateful for loyal supporters who stand with you through times of opposition.

This does not mean you can never disagree with the pastor, but if you do, it should be a private discussion, conducted in a respectful manner. Most issues can be resolved with honest discussion and candor in communication. If it becomes necessary to disassociate with a church or pastor, it should be done in a proper manner. You should be able to part on good terms, continue in fellowship, and be able to see one another at district meetings without regrets over attitudes or actions that erupted from angry confrontation.

Dedicated in Leadership

Joshua was dedicated to the house of God and to the work of the Lord. He was a frequent resident of the tabernacle as a young man. He loved the house of God.

> So the LORD spoke to Moses face to face, as a man speaks to his friend. And he would return to the camp, *but his servant Joshua the son of Nun, a young man, did not depart from the tabernacle* (Exodus 33:11).

Dedication to the house of God and the work of God is noted by others who will witness your dedication. Opportunities come to those who are noticed for their dedication. Recall how Phillip and six others in the early church were chosen to take care of the business because they "men of *good* reputation, full of the Holy Spirit and wisdom" (Acts 6:3). *These are still excellent qualities to find in an assistant!*

Passion in Leadership

On one occasion while Israel was camped in the wilderness, there were two Hebrews out in the camp prophesying on their own, away from the seventy elders gathered at the tabernacle. Joshua, desiring to protect the integrity of those at the tabernacle, called for them to be censured. Moses noted his passion for the right, but did not agree with Joshua's judgment. Moses desired for more people to become prophets working in the Spirit. Joshua had good intentions but was wrong in his assumption. When assistants or young ministers want to do something that would be harmful or unwise, a gentle correction, mixed with affirmation, will help them to grow and still allow the passion for ministry to thrive.

> So Joshua the son of Nun, *Moses' assistant, one of his choice men,* answered and said, "Moses my lord, forbid them!" Then Moses said to him, "Are you zealous for my sake? Oh, that all the Lord's people were prophets and that the LORD would put His Spirit upon them!" (Numbers 11:28-29).

Responsibility in Leadership

The Book of Numbers gives insight into a crucial role of responsibility Joshua and his counterpart, Caleb, played in the spying out of the land of Canaan. Among the twelve spies selected to secretly enter Canaan to ascertain the strength of the land and what opposition to expect, there were Joshua and Caleb.

> These are the names of the men whom Moses sent to *spy out the land.* And Moses called *Hoshea the son of Nun, Joshua* (Numbers 13:16).

While all the spies that entered Canaan are named in Scripture, very few have made the effort to remember them. Any student of the Bible can name the two men who gave a positive report of faith. Joshua and Caleb stood alone in the minority when giving this report.

> If the LORD delights in us, then *He will bring us into this land and give it to us,* "a land which flows with milk and honey" (Numbers 14: 8).

Sometimes, when standing for your convictions, you are in the minority. It takes a lot more courage to remain faithful to your beliefs when the polls are against you. It takes valor to speak truth when you know it will not be well received. Truth is easy to proclaim when singing to the choir, but the mark of a true *preacher* is when he proclaims the gospel to a spiritually tone-deaf audience.

Though eighty-three percent of the spies (ten of the twelve) declared that taking the land of Canaan was impossible, Joshua and Caleb were resolved that God would give them the land regardless of the obstacles. The people were swayed by the majority. They cried out in bitter despair that they had come so far from Egypt, only to face defeat in the conquest of Canaan. The judgment of God was pronounced on Israel with the decree that all from twenty years of age and over would die in the wilderness and they would not enter the Promised Land. God promised that they would wander in the wilderness for forty years, one year for every day the spies were in Canaan.

The one grand exception for the judgment that would come on all the people of Israel was these two faithful spies that said, "God can." Joshua and Caleb were exempted from the death sentence of the desert and promised that they would enter the Promised Land. It was their reward of faith—a reward for convictions kept.

> The carcasses of you who have complained against Me shall fall in this wilderness, all of you who were numbered, according to your entire number, from twenty years old and above. '_Except for Caleb the son of Jephunneh and Joshua the son of Nun,_ you shall by no means enter the land which I swore I would make you dwell in (Numbers 14:29-30).

When you refuse to give in to unbelief and fear, there is a promise of faith; _you shall live!_ When you follow after God and live by faith, the minority becomes the majority. Eventually, unbelievers will be gone and only the faithful will remain. In Noah's day there were only eight humans onboard the ark. In their generation they were the distinct minority—until _after_ the flood!

Now the men whom Moses sent to spy out the land, who returned and made all the congregation complain against him by bringing a bad report of the land, those very men who brought the evil report about the land, died by the plague before the LORD. *But Joshua the son of Nun and Caleb the son of Jephunneh remained alive,* of the men who went to spy out the land (Numbers 14:36-38).

When the faithless generation of Israel was dead in the wilderness sands of Sinai, Joshua and Caleb were two old men of faith among a new generation of believers. Your faith will inspire others to believe in the message you proclaim!

Transference of Leadership

When the time comes for leadership to be transferred, it should be done by seeking God and following Him. Few of us adequately prepare for our replacement. As pastors we sometimes feel immortal, as though we will always be here, leading the church, casting the vision, and making important decisions. But as surely as the day we were born, there is another day in the distance, the day we will pass from this life. True success in ministry is to do what you can do to insure that the work continues on after you are gone.

Then Moses spoke to the LORD, saying: 'Let the LORD, the God of the spirits of all flesh, set a man over the congregation, who may go out before them and go in before them, who may lead them out and bring them in, that the congregation of the LORD may not be like sheep which have no shepherd.

And the LORD said to Moses: '*Take Joshua the son of Nun with you, a man in whom is the Spirit,* and lay your hand on him; set him before Eleazar the priest and before all the congregation, and inaugurate him in their sight. And you shall give some of your authority to him, that all the congregation of the children of Israel may be obedient (Numbers 27:15-20).

Often a senior pastor will wish to bring a younger man into the ministry of a church with the intention of "turning it over" to him in the future. Sometimes this is expressed, but often it is only implied. When there is no clear communication of this intent, there is room for a lot of misunderstandings. In some cases the older minister fully intends to transfer the church to the young man, but when the excitement of someone new ignites a renewed passion for soul winning and evangelism in the church, the elder decides to stay a while longer. "Pastoring isn't so bad after all," he thinks. After a while, the younger minister moves on in disappointment, feeling that he was deceived and used.

If it is the intention of the senior pastor to transfer the church to the younger minister coming in, there should be a clear communication of those plans. Place your intentions in writing. Record the expectations and obligations of both parties. Outline a time frame of when each step of the transition will take place. If a young man knows up front that it will be five years, he will work more diligently knowing there is a goal and an objective for his involvement.

If there is no clear communication that there will be a transition, do not assume there will be. Assume that you are there until you feel God wants you somewhere else, or until there is clear direction for the future. Don't allow yourself to daydream the scene, "If I was the pastor here ...." It may never happen.

The Epithet of a Faithful Assistant

> Now Joshua the son of Nun was *full of the spirit of wisdom*, for Moses had laid his hands on him; so the children of Israel heeded him, and did as the LORD had commanded Moses. (Deuteronomy 34:9).

In this story, the assistant got the job. He became the leader in Moses' stead. This example serves as a model for ministry and the transference of leadership.

Other Biblical Examples for Assistants

There are a number of examples in Scripture of successful relationships between mentors and their assistants. Elijah was permitted to pick his successor, Elisha. He promised Elisha the mantle of anointing if he stayed with him until he was taken away. Nothing could shake the resolve of Elisha, and he was there with mouth agape as a chariot of fire swooped up Elijah before his eyes, and he boldly grasped the mantle that floated down from the ascending chariot.

Jesus had twelve assistants. He spent the majority of His ministry mentoring them. Eleven of them would be crucial to the promulgation of His vision. He commissioned His disciples to "Go into all the world and preach the gospel to every creature" (Mark 16:15). The success of His entire plan of redemption rested in the hands and hearts of twelve unpredictable men! And, it worked! Every gospel-preaching church in the world today had its beginning in the mentoring of the Twelve. Can we follow His example and mentor men that will do more than we will ever accomplish?

Paul trained Timothy in the work of the gospel. Part of his training manual we have as Scripture. The two letters to Timothy serve as a model for mentoring in ministry. Paul recognized the faith that was instilled in Timothy by his mother, Eunice, and his grandmother, Lois (2 Timothy 1:5). Paul instructed Timothy to preach the word, to do the work of an evangelist, and to fulfill his ministry (2 Timothy 4:2-5). *More of his instructions are recorded in the verses at the beginning of this chapter* (page 209). Paul's commendation to the Philippians was that Timothy had a "proven character, that as a son with his father he served with me in the gospel" (Philippians 2:22). To the Corinthians, Paul wrote that Timothy was "my beloved and faithful son in the Lord" (1 Corinthians 4:17). Might we accomplish more if there is such a relationship between pastor and assistant?

In a small or emerging church there are often not enough resources to pay someone to come in as an assistant. The pastor may be struggling financially and the church may be unable to meet its obligations. How can you get the help that you need to grow the church? Often we overlook the obvious. The needed talents are sometimes in our own backyard. When you begin to train and mentor those who are in your congregation, eventually you have assistants, Sunday school teachers, musicians, and soul winners. They didn't come with any qualifications, just a desire to work for the Lord. When we utilize the talents of those God brings to us, they grow into useful workers for God and find fulfillment in their own calling and ministry.

A pastor should not limit his search for someone to assist him to the men in the congregation. Just because there may not be a man available, don't overlook the fact that there may be women in the congregation that can fill a position of ministerial responsibility. There are many women around the world who fill positions of ministry in churches and do a superb job. Many women are available to serve and are just waiting to be asked. They only need to be given the permission and the authority to branch out into a new area of ministry.

While it may be tempting to look elsewhere and wish you could *afford* to bring in an assistant, a youth pastor, or a music director, remember that God has brought you the people you minister to. It could be that all the needs you have can be fulfilled by training and equipping them for ministry.

12

Pastor & Evangelist Relationships

And He Himself gave some to be apostles, some
prophets, some evangelists, and some pastors and
teachers, for the equipping of the saints for the work of
ministry, for the edifying of the body of Christ, till we
all come to the unity of the faith and of the knowledge
of the Son of God, to a perfect man, to the measure of
the stature
of the fullness of Christ.
—Ephesians 4:11-13

In an ideal world every evangelist would have
previously pastored and every pastor would have
evangelized. This creates a real *catch-22* situation. Even
if you were to have both experiences, you must do one
first and lack the experience of the other.

It is impractical to assume that anyone could have
done it all. We must learn a few lessons along the way

from the experiences of others. To walk a mile in someone else's shoes is to come to an understanding of his perspectives, feelings, and needs.

The Work of an Evangelist

> But you be watchful in all things, endure afflictions, *do the work of an evangelist,* fulfill your ministry (2 Timothy 4:5).

What is the work of an evangelist? Some view the evangelist as the one to call when you have newcomers who have not received the Holy Spirit. Others call an evangelist when they sense that the morale of the congregation is down and they need someone to get them *fired-up.* Still others see the evangelist as a *substitute preacher* so the pastor can get a break from his weekly routine of teaching and preaching. While all these may be true at times, the following aspects should outline the work of the contemporary evangelist.

- **Preach to reach the lost.** The evangelist should be able to minister to the unconverted, the visitor, or those who have not received the Spirit. *Evangelistic* preaching brings conviction of sin and faith in God. It is the preaching of the gospel "not with persuasive words of human wisdom, but in demonstration of the Spirit and of power, that your faith should not be in the wisdom of men but in the power of God" (1 Corinthians 2:4-5).

226

- **Preach to encourage and inspire the church.** There are some churches where there will be no visitors, no unbelievers present in the revival service. Preach faith and encourage the people and they will want to bring others out to experience the power of God. Refrain from berating or belittling the congregation for their lack of passion or blaming them because there are no *sinners* present.

- **Be passionate about revival.** If you are excited about revival and the refreshing of the Spirit in the church, others will get the same excitement and share your passion. Enthusiasm begets enthusiasm. If you are down and depressed it will be very hard to get anyone else encouraged!

- **Love the unconverted and the believer.** The evangelist must love people. If you don't love the unconverted, they will feel your lack of love and see you as a fake. If you don't love the believer, they may respect you but they will not respond to your ministry like they will when they feel your love toward them. Love cannot be manufactured. You must fall in love with Jesus so that His love will shine through you.

- **Leave a church better than you found it.** So, you may not be able to have one hundred new converts in every revival, but you can minister to the church and still have a victorious meeting. If you can leave a church a little better

227

off than it was when you rolled into town, you are a success. You will never know the eternal impact of a meeting.

- **Be an encouragement to the pastor and ministry of the local church.** You can be an encourager. Your passion for God will encourage other young ministers to follow after their calling. When a pastor sees his congregation and other ministers responding to your ministry, he is encouraged. When you are a blessing to a church, *you are invited back!*

The Evangelist's Responsibilities

Following are some guidelines developed from our years in the evangelistic ministry. This is by no means an exhaustive list of responsibilities, but it is a highlight of essential ethics for the evangelist in his or her relationship with pastors.

1. Respect the pastor.

The evangelist must have a high regard for the pastor of the local church. He should esteem him before the congregation and always show respect. While one ministry is not elevated above the other, it is always ethical to honor and give preference to one another (Romans 12:10). If you sow respect and honor you will reap the same.

Never allow members of the congregation to complain about the pastor to you. Always be supportive of the pastor in your comments to any member of the congregation. Some will try to get you to listen to their complaints about the pastor. It may start off innocently as a compliment to your ministry, *"We've never heard such wonderful preaching ... !"*

It is best to avoid invitations to eat out or to participate in any activity with members of the church *without* the pastor being present. If the pastor arranges the dinner or other activity, that is fine, but you should try to make sure he is included. When you are invited by a well-meaning member, you can respond with, "Have you checked to see if Pastor is available? I'm not sure what he has planned for us."

2. Respect the pastor's ministry.

The pastor is God's man for the local church congregation. He will be there working with his people long after the evangelist has gone down the road. An evangelist should support the ministry of the pastor and do his best to make his job easier.

The evangelist should avoid preaching personal convictions to another man's congregation. Each of us has our own convictions, standards of modesty, and viewpoints on a variety of issues. When preaching as a visiting minister it is best to stick to Bible doctrines and basic tenets of the faith. You should avoid preaching your personal feelings in areas that are not generally accepted by the fellowship. You will only create tension and disharmony by imposing your standard on a church where you are the visiting preacher.

There are ample topics in the Bible about sin, faith, salvation, grace, holiness, the oneness of God, redemption, etc. You will never run out of preaching material as long as you use the Bible as your sourcebook. It is right to preach on morality, integrity, and honesty. You can preach on holiness without naming specific standards that are different from church to church. You can preach on clean-living *without cleaning out the church!*

3. Respect the pastor's congregation.

The evangelist must care about people. There is a popular saying that states, "People don't care how much you know, until they know how much you care." If you really care, the congregation will feel it, the visitor will feel it, and the pastor will feel it. If you *don't care,* they will feel that also!

If you care, you will carry a burden that will be expressed in your ministry. When you preach on hell, people will know you don't want them to go there. When you preach about heaven they will know that you want them to be there. A hard, arrogant, "devil may care" attitude has NO PLACE in the ministry, especially for the evangelist.

4. Respect the pastor's calling.

The pastor has been called of God and placed in a position of trust and responsibility. When he invites an evangelist, he assumes responsibility to provide for the needs of this minister. When you trust the pastor, you trust his calling. Essentially, it is trusting God. The same God called both of you. He will work through the evangelist to bring spiritual renewal in the congregation.

230

He will work through the congregation and the pastor to provide the financial and physical needs of the evangelist.

You can trust God with your finances, your scheduling, your results, and your future. He did not call you to fail. He only calls successes. God cares more about His church than you ever will. He cares more about the "results" than we will. He has a plan for your life and will open doors of opportunity for you as you learn obedience and trust.

The Pastor's Responsibilities

The pastor also has some responsibilities to the evangelist or guest preacher that he invites to minister to his congregation. There are some basic areas of ethical treatment the pastor must keep in mind:

1. Be considerate of an evangelist's schedule.

If you insist that the evangelist come at a particular time that requires him to make a special trip across the country, be willing to pay his expenses. Otherwise, invite him to come when he is traveling in your state. If you invite him to call "when you're in our area" -- MEAN IT. Every evangelist has heard that line on numerous occasions when the pastor was not sincere, or perhaps, changed his mind.

If you only want the evangelist to come for a weekend service, be willing to wait until the evangelist can work it into an open week. If he reserves a weekend for you, he may have to sacrifice a week of revival to fulfill your invitation. The difference is financial. For a weekend engagement, you normally don't pay the same as you would for a week of special services. A slap on the back and a hearty, "God bless you!" doesn't pay the bills and fill the tank with gas. There are some definite financial obligations the pastor assumes when inviting an evangelist.

If you have an outstanding meeting and wish the evangelist to stay over for an extended revival, he may have to rearrange his schedule. Hopefully, other pastors will be willing to give up their evangelist for a spiritual breakthrough in your congregation. Remember this when a pastor or an evangelist asks you to do the same when they have a great breakthrough at the church prior to yours.

Most evangelists try to maintain a certain flexibility in their schedules. If you get cut out of the schedule at the appointed time, don't be upset and refuse to have him come at another time. Be flexible and be willing to accommodate this vital ministry and what it can offer your church.

2. Be considerate of an evangelist's time.

For the maximum benefit from a revival effort, allow the evangelist sufficient time each day for prayer, study, and preparation for the evening service. He may not tell you that he would rather not go fishing or golfing all day and barely have time to get changed before church. We all enjoy being entertained, but don't feel like that is an essential part of the revival meeting. If it is mutually agreed, save the special entertainment of the evangelist for a day off from revival services when there is no meeting scheduled in the evening.

3. Be considerate of an evangelist's income.

Money is always a hot topic when it comes to ministry. A church and a pastor should plan ahead for the financial aspect of revival just as you may plan the outreach or spiritual preparation of the church. A traditional evangelist makes his living on the road. Though he may not have the normal expenses of maintaining a house (many do), he has unusual expenses relating to travel. If he travels in a recreational vehicle there is considerable expense in insurance, maintenance, and fuel.

There are some weeks that cannot be scheduled for an evangelist. Camp meetings, conferences, major holidays, and *hunting season* (in some areas) are traditionally lean times for the fulltime evangelist. When the evangelist doesn't preach, he has no income unless a thoughtful pastor sends an  offering or pays extra for such a situation. Some districts have a financial plan that subsidizes an evangelist's income for the week so he may attend General Conference.

The tithe is the Lord's. The pastor must recognize that the evangelistic ministry is a part of the plan of God for the perfecting of the saints and this ministry should share the benefit of the tithing. If God has blessed you with abundance, look for an evangelist or a missionary to bless in return.

4. Be considerate of an evangelist's special needs.

If the evangelists travel in recreational vehicles, there may be special needs for utility hookups. They will need a heavier electrical circuit in order to use the A/C or other appliances. Some larger RV's may need a 220-volt electrical outlet. Try to find out what their needs are and prepare to accommodate them in advance.

They may need access to a phone. Not the one down the street in front of the local convenience store! This was one of the most pressing needs before the advent of cell phones. He may still need a phone line or a computer made available for internet access.

Some may have health concerns or need to contact a local doctor in case of illness, but are reluctant to ask for assistance. Remember that they are new in town and do not know the local businesses nor where to find the various services. The visiting evangelist may need diesel, propane, a drycleaners, the Post Office, the library, or the location of the shopping mall. It is helpful to create a sociable atmosphere where guests will feel free to ask if there are needs that you have been unable to anticipate.

Consider creating a map of your area with many of these locations clearly marked. You could also collect brochures of local interest to tourists. Have them available in the evangelist's quarters or in a packet to pass on to evangelists, missionaries, and other visitors when they come to town.

The Evangelist on the Road

While traveling as an evangelist from one church to another, you tend to hear all the local _news_. You must be careful not to carry gossip from one pastor's home to another. Many times you will be told things that you are just _dying_ to tell someone else. It is best to keep it to yourself until you hear the rest of the story. Sometimes when you hear the other side of a situation, new understanding comes and it doesn't sound so bad after all! As a general rule, if it is going to hurt someone or has a malicious intent, it is gossip and it should not be repeated. If your information does not edify, build up, strengthen, and encourage, it may be best to keep it to yourself. Check these three things before you repeat anything about someone else.

- Does it edify the person you are talking about?
- Does it edify the person you are telling it to?
- Does it edify Christ?

Therefore let us pursue the things which make for peace and the things by which one may _edify another_ (Romans 14:19).

Therefore comfort each other and _edify one another_, just as you also are doing (1 Thessalonians 5:11).

Be considerate of the pastor's time. The life of the pastor and his family goes on even during revival. Many have to work full-time jobs and pastor at the same time.

This may make it difficult to entertain you as a guest every night after church. Others pastor full-time and devote the days of the revival to the needs of the evangelist. The spectrum of diversity is wide. You will not be able to anticipate what any one pastor's family will do. When you arrive, the best plan is to ask what their desires are.

If you have a trailer, it would be easy to lock yourself away and deprive your host and hostess of your company. Refrain from enjoying your privacy so much that you forget to be a blessing to the pastor and his wife on a social level.

After service each night of a revival, many pastors invited my husband and me to go to a restaurant or to their home for a time of fellowship. Many times I was tired and my children were ready to go to bed, but my husband would lovingly remind me that this part of our ministry was as important as praying in the altar with sinners, or singing a special during the service. I knew his conviction was right. We were now moving into the most important part of our ministry—ministering to the ministry.

Many pastors and their wives live in remote cities that have no close churches with which to fellowship. These ministers and their wives need the fellowship of people of "like faith," and "like ministry." Being a pastor and wife can be a lonely life in these areas because of the caution needed in making casual friends with the congregation. The pastor and his wife need someone they can talk to, someone in whom they can confide. They have to be careful to guard their responsibility to the flock God has given them. There are some things a pastor or his wife

Pastor & Evangelist Relationships

cannot discuss with a member of the congregation. It is possible to become too common with a member, crippling his confidence in the ministry. If the pastoral couple have no other ministers in their church with which they can *let their hair down*, evangelists are refreshing ministerial friends. With an evangelist they can laugh, cry, and enjoy wonderful times of fellowship.

In contrast with pastors who need and welcome your fellowship long into the night, there are those who cannot spend the time with you for various reasons. A full-time job may keep a pastor busy during the day. By the time he gets home, eats supper, and attends church, he is exhausted and just wants to go to bed. By all means, honor this without offense. It is not because they don't *want* to spend the time with you; it is because they don't *have* the time to spend with you. If you are visiting after church over some coffee or small snack and you notice the pastor's wife nodding off, a simple suggestion of your wish to retire may be just the relief she needs. Their obligations do not stop when you pull into town. Daily schedules, meetings, phone calls, school, and other responsibilities continue for the pastor and his wife *in addition* to the revival. It is a wonderful virtue to practice sensitivity to their lifestyle.

If you are staying in the pastor's home, try to keep your room neat and tidy, making your bed each morning. It is a challenge to live out of a suitcase, but if you practice the discipline of putting your clothes away immediately after undressing, it will help keep your area clean.

Whether you share the main bathroom with others of the household or you have your own private one, it is good to be sensitive about keeping it clean also. Do not store your toiletries in a bathroom that others will be using, unless the hostess insists or has a small storage area vacant for the guests' things. Ask the lady of the house what to do with damp towels. Some wash each towel after a single use; others use a towel several times before washing it.

The Evangelist as a Dinner Guest

When an evangelist arrives at the place he is preaching, it is understood that the pastor will take care of him while he is there. This is usually the case, but on occasion, if there is an oversight on the pastor's part, it will be less embarrassing if you are prepared. Never presume you will be taken care of exclusively. Keep some food on hand or cash available if you arrive and find no arrangements for dinner the first night. Some pastors prefer to eat after church, if the schedule does not allow a before-service dining experience.

Dining Out

When the pastor asks the evangelist out to dinner, it is with the understanding that the pastor will pay for the meal. When seated, if he suggests that you order first, you should not order one of the most expensive items on the menu unless the pastor makes a suggestion, indicating that it is all right. You may put him in an embarrassing situation if you order an expensive entrée with an appetizer and dessert. He may not have the money to cover the expenses. If he says something like, "I think you would enjoy the filet mignon. It is a specialty here," or

238

"I'm going to have cheesecake. Would you like dessert too?" It is then alright to order that item. Sensitivity to the financial needs of your host is a gracious gesture that will be well rewarded with repeated invitations.[36]

Dining in the Pastor's Home

It is a generous gesture to be asked to dine in the pastor's home. The evangelist is a guest, but at the same time he is serving the pastor and his wife in a position of ministry.[37] When the evangelist's wife offers her services to the pastor's wife during the preparation of the meal, it shows that she is ready to help share the load. Some pastors' wives feel comfortable with this while others do not. It is up to the evangelist's wife to ask if she can help in order to find out what her limitations and liberties are in another woman's kitchen. Some pastors' wives feel more comfortable with the clean-up afterward, rather than the preparations before dinner. Whatever the case, if a little help is offered, it shows that the evangelist and his wife are willing to serve others.

If your family has health issues or if you are allergic to certain foods, it is good to let the pastor know before the first meal, if possible. Leaving large portions of uneaten food on your plate may indicate you are a picky eater to your host and ungrateful for their hospitality. Rather than cause hurt feelings at the dinner table, it is better to communicate your needs up front.

---

[36] Baughman, *Christian Social Graces*, 328-329.
[37] Ibid, 342.

Single Evangelist Dating

It is a natural thing for a single evangelist to be interested in finding a wife. The opportunities may seem limitless while traveling from church to church, but he must be very careful how he conducts his dating routine. The evangelist's reputation and integrity should be a priority at all times. Young ministers should not feel that dating is prohibited while evangelizing, but they should proceed with caution, setting guidelines with accountability and keeping an impeccable reputation while preaching in another man's pulpit.

The evangelist should always ask the permission of the pastor before dating a young lady in his church. Asking the pastor's permission has several advantages.

1. If the pastor knows of any problems that she has had, he could discretely discourage you from being involved in what might become an embarrassing situation.

2. It is usually a good sign when the pastor approves of a young woman from his church. If he gives his consent, it is usually with the understanding that the young lady would be compatible to your ministry.

3. Asking the pastor's permission gives you an opportunity to invite the pastor and his wife to come along!

It would be wise to refrain from dating alone as a couple until you are ready to commit to a serious relationship. There is a *third-party* rule at the college where we teach. A third person serves as a chaperone—a safeguard for a couple. The third-party rule has several advantages. Not only does it help protect young ladies from being taken advantage of, but it also helps maintain a good reputation, an essential quality for young men and women going into the ministry. A third-party may also be a valued witness in case any false accusations are made concerning one's conduct on a date.

Group dating is a fairly safe environment to get to know a young woman while in revival. When going out with a group of young people the environment is more relaxed with others around to join in the conversation. There is "safety in numbers" and your reputation is protected when you are out with a crowd. You have plenty of *witnesses* to your behavior with a young lady when you are in a group.

To avoid the label of a *player,* it is important that you refrain from flirting with all the young ladies in the church. The integrity of the evangelist is vital to the success of the revival. Others will have difficulty responding to the message, if the messenger has difficulty controlling his actions around women.

Whatever you do in public will reflect on your ministry. It is imperative that your reputation be above reproach in the area of dating relationships. There should be no physical contact with a young lady during a revival. Take care to guard your reputation from any misinterpretation of your actions with a member of the opposite sex.

Some evangelists choose to refrain from dating at all while conducting services in the home churches of those they are interested in. After the revival is over, they may spend their time off pursuing the lady of choice.

With new technology, such as e-mail and cell phones, long distance relationships are much easier to maintain today than they were several years ago. Once the evangelist is out of town, keeping in contact with a young lady is considered long-distance dating. Although it may not have been their first choice, many ministers who found their companions while evangelizing can attest to the fact that long-distance dating is better than no dating at all.

Conclusion

Finally then, brethren, we urge and exhort
in the Lord Jesus that you should abound
more and more, just as you received from us
how you ought to walk and to please God.
—1 Thessalonians 4:1

By observing practical guidelines and ethical behavior the minister can enjoy a wonderful relationship with pastors and others in ministry for years to come. This blessing will also be extended to many other relationships as he or she enjoys the sweet fruit of a well-tended tree of integrity and faithfulness.

Though at times you may feel that others can violate ethics, ignore etiquette, and even be immoral, and yet succeed in ministry, there is a reckoning day. A person's lifestyle will eventually catch up with him. If he flaunts his liberty and scorns propriety, someday others will see his duplicity.

Therefore *whatever you have spoken in the dark* will be heard in the light, and what you have spoken in the ear in inner rooms will be *proclaimed on the housetops* (Luke 12:3).

It is vital that we live our lives in such as way as to look in the mirror without shame and face all men without fear of exposure. To be at peace with God and man brings the ultimate fulfillment.

This above all: to thine own self be true,
And it must follow, as the night the day,
Thou canst not then be false to any man.
Farewell; my blessing season this in thee!

-- William Shakespeare, *Hamlet*

Ministerial Resources

A wise man will hear and increase learning,
And a man of understanding
will attain wise counsel.
—Proverbs 1:5

Funeral Resources

Al Cadenhead. *The Ministers Manual for Funerals.* (Nashville: Broadman and Holman), 1988.

Fred J. Foster. *Foster's Ministry Manual.* (West Monroe, LA: Twin Cities University), 1996.

Victor D. Lehman. *The Pastor's Guide to Weddings & Funerals.* (Valley Forge, PA: Judson Press), 2001.

C.S. Lewis. *A Grief Observed.* (New York: Harpercollins Publishing), 1989.

T.F. Tenney. *Beyond the Sunrise, A collection of funeral sermons and thoughts.* (Tioga, LA: Focused Light Publications), 1995.

Warren W. Wiersbe & David W. Wiersbe. *Comforting the Bereaved,* (Chicago: Moody Press) 1985.

Wedding Resources

Gayla M. Baughman. *To Have And To Hold, Wedding Planner.* (Pleasanton, CA: Baughman Group), 2002.

Jerry D. Hardin & Dianne C. Sloan. *Getting Ready for Marriage Workbook, How to Really Get to Know the Person You're Going to Marry.* (Nashville: Thomas Nelson), 1992.

S.W. Hutton. *Minister's Service Manual, updated and expanded.* (Grand Rapids: Baker), 2003.

Tim and Beverly LaHaye. *The Act of Marriage and the Beauty of Sexual Love.* (Grand Rapids: Zondervan), 1998.

Victor D. Lehman. *The Pastor's Guide to Weddings & Funerals.* (Valley Forge, PA: Judson Press), 2001.

Louis & Melissa McBurney. *Real Questions, Real Answers about Sex: The Complete Guide to Intimacy as God Intended.* (Grand Rapids: Zondervan), 2004.

H. Norman Wright. *The Pre-marital Counseling Handbook.* (Chicago: Moody Publishers), 1992.

H. Norman Wright and Wes Roberts. *Before You Say "I Do," revised.* (Eugene, OR: Harvest House), 1997.

Gary Smalley. Hidden Keys of a Loving, Lasting Marriage. (Grand Rapids: Zondervan), 1993.

Dennis Rainey. *Preparing for Marriage.* (Ventura, CA: Gospel Light), 1997.

Dennis & Barbara Rainey. *Starting Your Marriage Right.* (Nashville: Thomas Nelson), 2000.

General Ministry Resources

Gayla Baughman. *Christian Social Graces: A Guide for the Pentecostal Woman.* (Pleasanton, CA: Baughman Group), 2001.

Terry R. Baughman, ed. *Third Millennium Ministry, Vol. 1.* (Stockton, CA: Christian Life College Press), 2004.

_____. *Grace is a Pentecostal Message,* (Pleasanton, CA: Baughman Group), 2002.

James D. Berkley, ed. *Leadership Handbook of Preaching and Worship.* (Grand Rapids: Baker), 1997.

_____. *Leadership Handbook of Outreach and Care.* (Grand Rapids: Baker), 1997.

Vickie Kraft and Gwynne Johnson. *Women Mentoring Women: Ways to Start, Maintain and Expand a Biblical Women's Ministry.* (Chicago: Moody Publishers), revised 2003.

Joe E. Trull & James E. Carter. *Ministerial Ethics: Moral Formation for Church Leaders.* (Grand Rapids: Baker Academic, 2004).

Other Resources Available

Christian Social Graces, for the Pentecostal Woman
by Gayla M. Baughman

Christian Social Graces is an etiquette book tailored for the Christian woman. Author Gayla Baughman stresses the importance of who you are and how to conduct yourself socially in areas of communication and hospitality etiquette, such as manners and the setting of a table. She also includes the proper etiquette involved in planning weddings and showers, as well as how to act as a guest in someone else's home and tips on being a proper hostess. The reader will be entertained and educated in the areas of various social graces as Gayla shares personal experiences mixed with traditional etiquette designed for Pentecostal women of all ages. (415 pages, 5½ x 8½)

ISBN 0-9710411-0-5   **USD $16.00**

Christian Social Graces Workbook
by Gayla M. Baughman

This workbook is the perfect companion for *Christian Social Graces: A Guide for the Pentecostal Woman* if you want to put its lessons into action. It is designed to reinforce the principles of Christian hospitality, communication, and other social graces with hands-on practical assignments and fill-in pages. It can be used as a self-help tool or as a student workbook for each one in a class setting. (120 pages, 8½x11)

ISBN 0-9710411-3-X   **USD $13.00**

To Have & To Hold - *Wedding Planner*
by Gayla M. Baughman

Are you planning a wedding? Whether it is your own special occasion or you are coordinating someone else's wedding, you won't want to be without this handy Wedding Planner. Gayla has drawn from the knowledge and experience of several professional Christian wedding coordinators to provide you with the best, most effective tool for your planning. This spiral-bound book is packed full of handy worksheets, organizational guides, time saving tips and many wonderful ideas with a Christian perspective to make your special day a memorable one. (160 pages, spiral, 5 ½ x 8 ½)

ISBN 0-9710411-1-3   **USD $12.50**

Let's Go! An Autobiography of Mark Baughman
with Terry R. Baughman

The story of a pioneer preacher, his conversion to Christ during depression years and the strong call of God on his life that led him from raising crops on an isolated Oklahoma farm, to labor in another harvest field across the country; the field of souls. He candidly reveals his personal struggles to fulfill God's call in the face of obstacles. You will sympathize with the struggles and rejoice in the victories as you journey through the pages of the lives of Mark and Zealous Baughman as they raise four children in evangelistic work and labor to build churches throughout the Southwest. (196 pages, 5½ x 8½)

Item 1-08524-563-2   **USD $11.00**

Mysteries of the Kingdom
by Terry R. Baughman

Jesus promised to reveal the "mysteries of the kingdom" to those that hear and believe his teaching in the parables. Jesus explained that an understanding of the mysteries of the kingdom of heaven was given to the disciples but concealed from those who rejected his message. *Mysteries of the Kingdom* is a study of the parables of Matthew 13 and what they reveal concerning the inclusion of Gentiles in the kingdom of heaven. (134 pgs, 5½ x 8½)

ISBN 0-9710411-5-6   **USD $12.00**

Preach It! *Selected Sermons of Mark Baughman*

Terry R. Baughman, Editor

Mark Baughman powerfully preached the Word of God for more than sixty-five years everywhere from street corners in small Oklahoma towns to the beautiful sanctuaries of some of the largest Pentecostal churches in the country. His expository development of sermons made him a favorite among Bible lovers everywhere he ministered, as the Word was brought to life by its commentary upon itself. This collection of sermons is divided into three topical sections: doctrinal, evangelistic, and prophecy. You will find these sermons to be solidly biblical and thought provoking. (248 pages, 5 ½ x 8 ½)

ISBN 0-9710411-2-1   **USD $12.00**

Grace is a Pentecostal Message

by Terry R. Baughman

Pentecost is powerful, experiential, and emotive, Common to the experience is the conviction that the enduing power of the Holy Spirit disqualifies dependence on Grace. All too often we have assigned Grace to another denomination with "less truth." In reality, we have expected the power of the Holy Ghost and obedience to the Word to produce something that can never be realized outside of total acceptance of God's great grace. Grace didn't come lately to Pentecost. It started here, in a *born-again experience* with a risen Savior. Grace *is* a Pentecostal message! (170 pages, 5 ½ x 8 ½)

ISBN 0-9710411-4-8   **USD $11.00**

Ethics & Etiquette: for Today's Ministry

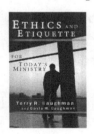

by Terry & Gayla Baughman

Addressing the vital subject of ministerial ethics with a fresh look, Terry R. Baughman compiles lessons and practical applications from the class on this subject at Christian Life College. Gayla Baughman joins in this project with her expertise in Christian social etiquette to produce this informative and insightful edition. It deals with the theoretical as well as the practical issues of proper conduct in the contemporary life of the ministry. (5 ½ x 8 ½)

ISBN 0-9710411-7-2   **USD $15.00**

Third Millennium Ministry, Vol. 1

Terry R. Baughman, general editor

Nine Christian Life College faculty members have contributed articles of varying subjects to engage your mind, stir your heart, and challenge you to greater commitment to ministry in the third millennium. In these pages, you will find articles of enduring substance: cultural challenges to ministry in the future of the church; discussion of the history of music ministry and current trends; examine the use of Hebrew Scripture in the New Testament; find inspiration for a writing ministry of your own; discover your gifts and develop your talents in women's ministry; feel the call for greater involvement in Christian service; evaluate the challenges to integration of psychology and theology; challenges of postmodernism in practicing spiritual disciplines; and experience a new dimension of prayer. (196 pages, 5 ½ x 8 ½)

ISBN 0-9710411-6-4   **USD $5.00**

To order these resources indicate number of each title desired and add shipping and handling charges:

____ copies of *Christian Social Graces* @ $16.00 ea. $_____

____ copies of *Social Graces **Workbook*** @ $13.00 ea. $_____

__ copies *To Have & To Hold, Wedding Planner* @ $12.50 ea. $_____

____ copies of *Let's Go! Mark Baughman* @ $11.00 ea. $_____

____ copies of *Mysteries of the Kingdom* @ $12.00 ea. $_____

____ copies of *Preach It! Selected Sermons* @ $12.00 ea. $_____

____ copies of *Grace is a Pentecostal Message* @ $11.00 ea. $_____

____ copies of *Ethic & Etiquette, today's ministry* @ $15.00 ea. $_____

____ copies of *Third Millennium Ministry, Vol.1* @ $5.00 ea. $_____

10% Shipping & Handling (20% Canadian/30% Foreign) $_____

***Total amount enclosed $**_____

– Address form on next page –

Gayla M. Baughman, author, songwriter and musician, is the director of Women's Ministries at *LifeChurch*, Gilbert, AZ. She was formerly an instructor at *Christian Life College,* Stockton, California, where she received a Bachelor of Arts in Christian Music. She taught a variety of courses including *Social Graces, Women's Ministries, Dating and Relationships,* and *Marriage and Family.* During her musical career she recorded four projects with her family, *The Bible Singing Bibb Family,* two choir projects with *Abundant Life Temple* in Gladewater, Texas, as well as three recordings with her husband since their marriage in 1979. As the mother of two grown children she has now turned to writing and speaking as additional outlets for ministry.

଼

Terry R. Baughman is the lead pastor of *LifeChurch,* Gilbert, AZ. He also serves as an adjunct faculty for *Christian Life College*, Stockton, California, where he teaches online and on campus. He earned a Bachelor of Arts in Bible and Theology from *Christian Life College* in 1977 and received his Master of Arts in Exegetical Theology in 1999 from *Western Seminary* in San Jose, California. A minister with the *United Pentecostal Church International* since 1976, he has evangelized throughout the Southwest, pastored *Truth Center* in Canyon, Texas, and founded *Worship & Word-the Northwest Church* in Peoria, Arizona and *The Pentecostals of Pleasanton,* California.

Please visit our website for current ordering information:
www.baughmangroup.org or
www.baughmangroupministries.com
Email: trbaughman@baughmangroup.org

Ship to: (Please Print)

Name		
Address		
City	**St**	**Zip**
Phone		
Email		

Your support of this ministry subsidizes international missions projects.